She Saw an Angel In Every Devil

The Resilience Of A Warrior

Crystal G. Cisco

She Saw an Angel In Every Devil

First Edition

Graphic art and design by Corie E. Nance

Library of Congress Cataloging-in Publication Data has been applied for.

ISBN: 979-8-9861851-0-1

Reviews

It was an inspiring book, I loved it! It was sad, but I really think in my own words that you're a strong woman. You're so positive about life after all you went through, this book will inspire millions of other women. Thank you so much for sharing. Crystal Locklear.

I have never been so caught up in a book, I literally forgot where I was. Girl, you put your heart and soul in this book. I felt every emotion you wrote to the point I felt like I was right there with you. I really enjoyed reading your book, and I believe this book will inspire many women. Kathy Melvin

A perfect walk-through hell and back! I'm still shocked in amazement! The authors sense of relief is felt at the end of each chapter. The chapter's named by song titles fit each chapter perfectly! If Rob Zombie and Janis Joplin had a child, it would be you girl! The feelings and emotions I felt reading your book could never be expressed it was such a great read. I couldn't stop reading until the end. Jeremy Gipson

"She Saw an Angel in Every Devil" could be one of those endless fictional Hollywood stories, bend from drama to excitement to please the audience. Because, real bad shit only happens in the movies, right? This story will pull you down to earth and rip you out of your illusion and realty. It makes you wonder what went wrong with our society, why do we look the other way? Instead of recognizing other's struggles and offer help! Crystal tells her story of pain and still delivered hope. I can't wait to read part 2! Mellody Still

This is a must read, I could not put it down. I have struggled with addiction most of my adult life. The way Crystal tells her story showed me there is hope and help is there when we are ready to accept it. Traci Suarez

An absolute masterpiece! Not only brilliant written, but I had the privileges of seeing all the hard work that went into writing this…. first hand. You defeated all odds, and I can't wait to see what the future has in store for this wonderful woman. Continue this positive path you are on and watch out! I can't wait for book #2! Love Always your best friend Sean!

This is an honest story of circumstances that would crumble most, persevered working through the pain life threw at her. She allows you to take a walk in her shoes experiencing the pain of addiction, heartbreak, and trauma caused by loving the wrong type of man. She leaves you with her journey to self-discovery, healing and most importantly love. Patricia Hampshire

I want to express my gratitude to all seven of my pre-reviewers. You didn't just read and show love towards my story, but you gave me confidence to grow even more in life! I know most of you from personal experiences and I love every one of you. I courage everyone to always stay positive through life. I promise you no matter how hard it seems the stars above us all will always guide us to the light!

Thank you so very much for walking side by side me while going through this beautiful journey. Crystal

Dedication

I want to dedicate my novel to my mother Cindy Lou Heffelbower, you're my hero, mom. I understand your madness in every way, and I know you did your best! You held down three jobs at a time and keeping us kids clean and fed. You lived your life the only way you were taught, and I no longer hold that against you, but now I understand you! I understand and believe you loved us all very much. I understand you were ashamed for some of your actions which threw your world upside down. Remembering the stories, you told me as a young girl about your own trauma gives me a better understanding of my own trauma. I love you mother and miss you dearly! You gave birth to a legend and warrior! I am the curse breaker, and I will continue making you proud!

Sean, I want to take this time and express my love for you. You have showed me a love I only dreamed of. Standing by my side and teaching me what a real man does when he truly loves a woman has brought so much peace within my heart. You're my rock and I cannot wait to become your wife. Love you, Hunny!

Editor's Letter /Introduction

This book had me captivated from page one. It is a gripping story about the life of a child growing up in a very cruel adult world and experiencing things she should never have been exposed to. I felt all the emotions and trauma that this poor woman had faced throughout her life. A very sad but true story that will pull at your heartstrings from the beginning to end.

Your story has inspired me. Thank you for allowing me to be part of your life story, I've been honored. I believe this book to be brilliant from beginning to end. This is a winner, Crystal. It's captivating and a brilliant read. You certainly had me hooked, I sat for hours, I couldn't seem to budge. I laughed with you, I cried with you. My heart even broke for you, this book is too much for one person to bear! I loved every chapter, every page, and every word. Your story is very inspiring, I just wanted to hold you and tell you everything would be ok. You are a hero, a survivor!

Foreword

This book was written as an autobiography novel, about my world. Growing up with monsters living underneath my bed gave me strength to survive the unthinkable. With willingness and grace, I was able to shine as bright as my favorite star in the sky. Although confused of the power I held as a young child, only pushed me to search for what I knew existed in Crystal's world, Love! I want my readers to understand through my story that healing isn't rainbows and butterflies, but with preservation and willingness greatness can and will happen. I went from a lost soul searching for love, to understanding loving oneself is the first step to a beautiful life. If no one in this world believes in you, please understand I do. If I can crawl out of the depths of hell after being pulled and dragged back down many times throughout my life, and stand brightly with peace in my soul, so can you. Madd love to all my reader's!

Crystal G. Cisco

Content/Playlist

1. Blood-By In This Moment

2. Unsteady-By X Ambassadors

3. Family Portrait-By Pink

4. Believer-By Imagine Dragons

5. Your Mama Don't Dance-By Poison

6. Janie's got a gun-By Aerosmith

7. I can't Make You Love Me-By Bonnie Rait

8. Til it Happens To You-By Lady Gaga

9. When The Doves Cry-By Prince

10. Down with the Sickness-By Disturb

11. I Miss The Days-By NF

12. Time After Time-By Cyndi Lauper

13. What About Your Friends-By T.L.C

14. This Is What Made Us Girls-By Lana Del Ray

15. Fuck The World-By 2Pac

16. Don't Let me be Misunderstood-By The Animals

17. King Cry Baby-By Johnny Depp

18. Gimme Shelter-By Rolling Stone

19. We Don't Need a Education-By Pink Floyd

20. Fight For Your Right-By Beastie Boys

21. Superman-By Eminem

22. 25 To Life- By Eminem

23. Love The Way You Lie part 2-By Eminem

24. Run-By Pink

25. Mockingbird-By Eminem

26. Simple Man-By Lynyrd Skynyrd

27. One-By Metallica

28. The House Of the Raising Sun-By The Animals

29. Thunderstruck-By AC/DC

30. Free Bird- By Lynyrd Skynyrd

31. Blue Jeans-By Lana Del Rey

32. Fuck Faces-By Scarface

33. Ex-Factor-By Lauryn Hill

34. Mirror-By Lil Wayne

35. You Broke me First-By Tate McRae

36. Spenda Little Doe-By Lil Kim

37. Why Did You Leave Us-By NF

38. I'm Sick of Trying-By Vaboh

39. Gangsta-By Kehlani

40.Needed Me-By Rihanna

41.Saddest Day- By Foxy Brown

42.Gods & Monsters-By Lana Del Rey

43.Serial Killer-By Lana Del Rey

44.Be Careful -By Cardi B

45.My Medicine-By The Pretty Reckless

46.Aunt Dot-By Lil Kim

47. The Purge-By Demetriusx

48.Whore-By In This Moment

49.Puff The Magic Dragon-By Peter & Mary

50. Too Good at Goodbyes-By Sam Smith

51.Ride-By Lana Del Rey

52.Adrenalize-By In This Moment

53.Is That Alright-By Lady Gaga

54. I need You-By Lynyrd Skynyrd

55.Shallow-By Lady Gaga

56.Save Me-By Jelly Roll

57.Always Remember us This Way-By Laday Gaga

58.Get You the Moon-By Kina

59. Rehab-By Amy Winehouse

CHAPTER 1

" BLOOD" In This Moment!

I was brought to this earth by the loins of the first man who walked out of my life, October 24th, 1979. My mother pushed with all her might, screaming so loud, I was told the whole floor heard her cries. I think back and wonder if those cries were from the pain of delivering a baby? Or were those torturous screams from the agony of her choices? Either way I was coming, and boy what a life was ahead of me. Buckle up, this is going to be a ride of a lifetime.

I was born 7 pounds and 2 ounces - a head full of coal black hair. The only words that fell out Cindy's mouth was "Oh shit." My aunt Daleen was standing next to her throughout the whole delivery, and there came Chris busting through the door, late. Cindy, pointing her finger, yelled, "Get the fuck out!" Chris was not just late but drunk. He was wearing the robe my grandmother bought for her daughter to wear after the delivery. My mom and aunt looked at one another and said, "This baby cannot be Chris's child." No one said a word. With so much commotion going on, Cindy signed my last name as Heffelbower - a strong German name, and her birth name too.

Growing up in a situation I was not asked to be involved in, was one of the hardest pills to swallow. Not knowing where it was going to lead me to in life, was frightening. I was five years of age, when I woke up to what was finally coming to light from the day I was born. All I could remember was my mom and dad yelling and crying in the early am, after bar time. I hid behind the wall confused as to why my parents were fighting. I saw my father's head in his hands - sitting on our couch crying.

Chris kept saying over and over, "How could you Cindy." My mother standing yelling back, "You knew she wasn't yours." This early morning confession changed my entire life in a matter of moments. I went back to bed looking at the stars twinkling through my window, thinking about what I had heard. Wondering how I knew exactly what Cindy said was true, that Chris wasn't my real father. I fell asleep with an aching heart, not for myself but for my dad, Chris.

The following morning, I went into the living room to find my father sitting quietly in a chair. I walked towards him and hugged him, "I don't care what mom said dad, you'll always be my real dad." He looked at me and gave me a huge hug, "What are you talking about Crystal? You will always be daddy's princess!" Those words never left my heart.

CHAPTER 2

"UNSTEADY" X Ambassadors.

Time went by and many more fights, like the one I heard that early am arose. Chris would drink his Budweiser until he was in a full-blown drunken state of mind -yelling and crying in front of company.

One night the whole Cisco family was out bowling. Our parents were drinking and the kids were running around the bowling alley, being children. I have a vivid memory of that night; it was the last night my family was whole. My father and mother got into their normal fight, but this time everything shattered like glass.

Chris started calling my mother a whore in front of the entire Cisco family. Time stood still that very moment. I remember feeling so embarrassed, asking myself why they couldn't love me without fighting about it?

My grandpa Max, a man of few words, stood up telling both my parents to shut their mouths He stated, "This has gone on way too long" and before he could go on, my father looked at him and broke down in tears, crying out loud, "She's not mine dad! How could she have done this to me."

They had forgotten that I was standing right there during the commotion. My mother grabbed my hand leaving my brother and sister behind, yelling, "I don't need you Chris," I will do this myself!

Chris heard it in her voice. He knew she was serious this time. He ran after her begging her to stay and apologized for making another scene. I was always put in the middle of these situations: my dad's hand wrapped around one arm and my mother's wrapped around the other arm. I was in a tug a war - Chris pleading his love to Cindy and me, and Cindy more fed up with every round, I felt life changing at that very moment.

CHAPTER 3

"FAMILY PORTRAIT" Pink

I ran off breaking loose from them both, my cousin running behind me. I found my first quiet place when I stopped. My cousin sat next to me and apologized for my parents' actions, after handing me my first Budweiser.

I shrugged my shoulders and grabbed the beer can, cracking it open and chugging it until there was nothing left to chug. I remember two things from that moment: I finally felt warmth from a bad situation, and I had no Fucks to give. I was five.

I was five when I was told the truth behind the tears of my father. I was five when my mother and us kids packed up our lives and drove away without Dad. I sat in the back of our old Volkswagen crying for my father and begging my mother to go back and get him from the middle of the road.

The further we drove, the more my heart crumbled for the man we left behind. I always knew Chris loved us. I knew the love of his life broke his heart in pieces that day. I know today it was not caused from the truth of me not being his biological daughter.

Knowing what I know today, I believe my father Chris; knew from the time I was born that I was not his child. The love Chris held in his heart for Cindy was so deep that he opened his heart and his family to me. Today I thank him daily for that type of love he was able to share with me. Today I understand that blood is not thicker than water, and in every angel, there is a devil.

That man gave me a beautiful life. His love saved my life in ways I am still yet to tell him. No matter the gene I share with the other biological half of me, I know the Cisco family tree gave me the heart I carry within me.

CHAPTER 4

"BELIEVER" Imagine Dragons

Mom found some freedom and a place for us to call home. We lived in these apartments that we were able to run freely, with the kids that also lived in the area. I quickly made friends and found various play spots that I ran to every time life seemed hard.

These spots might seem morbid for some, but they gave me a peace of mind. There was a creek that ran behind the apartments and surrounding this creek was trees for me to explore through. Next to this forest of wonder was a cemetery I would go to, to speak to the dead. Yeah, I know, I was a strange kid.

I would wander down this bike path I found, as fast as I could pedal my little legs, and as soon as I felt the speed creating the wind that melted in my skin and ran its fingers through my hair, I knew I was going to be ok. The rush and peace I found in that type of creation was beautiful to my soul.

I always raise one arm if not both arms, to the universe to feel every bit of its magic. Yes, even though a wreck of a life, I have always found the beauty in this world. I used to call it a beautiful curse. Today I know it is a blessing. The freedom

I felt during those moments were a preview from the universe. Growing up outside, playing, was the greatest times as a child. Even though they did not last long, I am always grateful for these types of memories. I believe it was what kept me going from what was about to happen in the near future.

Things seemed peaceful at first. Mom enrolled us into school, and we made friends quickly. Then we went to bed one night, woke up, and once again our world was about to change. I had no clue what and how to deal with the madness heading our way. I had no clue how to save any of us from the pain the world was handing us all. To be honest that is all I wanted to do: help my family. I wanted so badly to save them all, but I was just a kid trying to be an adult.

CHAPTER 5

"YOUR MOMMA DON'T DANCE" Poison

My mother's freedom quickly turned into a horror flick. She was going out to parties on a regular basis. Between taking care of a household, raising three little kids, plus holding down a full-time job, I'm guessing she was looking for a little bit of excitement.

She did not know her need for excitement was the start of my childhood trauma. Mom's glass table was usually full of straws and cocaine left behind from the night before friends. After many nights of these accuracies, I became the maid, mother, and friend of the house.

Worried about what time my mother would make it home I started losing sleep. Losing sleep meant not making it to school on time, and not making it to school meant getting my ass kicked. So, mom started partying more at home. That's when I started noticing my mother's mental state disconnecting from reality. She met this man named Steve-what a fucking douche bag. He was fourteen years older than her and sold lots of what they called 'Reefer' back then. He was in a blues band, and he knew a lot more about life than my mother did. To her, he was a God sent from the heavens above. I knew right away that he was a piece of dog shit.

That did not stop Cindy from falling for him. Matter of fact, when Dick on the stick said the sky was green, mom believed every word that fell out that man's mouth. At first, she seemed happy she was able to move on from my dad. Shortly after her and Steve became a couple, she noticed his sneaky ways. She wasn't a woman that kept her mouth shut, so when she confronted him about his disloyalty, he would beat her.

Every other weekend my dad would come pick us up, and that is when Steve would beat the fuck out of my mom. We came home on a Sunday, and her bedroom door would be shut and locked.

I knew something was wrong, I started knocking at the door asking her to let me in. I could hear her cries from the other side of the door. I begged her to just open the door. When I finally got her to open up, I could not believe my eyes. She was black and blue, and her face was swollen. It was so bad that she looked like she was hit by a semi.

I asked, "Mom, what happened to you?" She lied to me and told me she had been in a car accident. I heard later while she was on the phone with one of her friends that Steve got caught cheating and when mom found him at the bar with this other chic, mom went nuts. So, Steve, being the narcissist he was, got my mother to calm down and brought her back home. He knew no one would be there, and that was his chance to get her alone to beat the living crap out of her. No one could see the true snake he was.

CHAPTER 6

"JANIE'S GOT A GUN" Aerosmith

I took care of my mother's wounds until she got herself back on her feet. She would look at me while I was changing out her ice pack and thanked me, "Crystal Gail, don't' ever let a man hit on you, do you hear me?"

Years of physical and mental abuse from the hands of the man that claimed he loved her, brought her to a world of disaster. I hated that man. I would stay up plotting this man's death, wishing I was big enough to take a bat to his head.

Anger wasn't the word for what I felt for this guy. Cindy did what 95% of women do when we feel comfortable with a shit head. She opened her door to madness; and our world of chaos began.

The longer she kept him around the more she became unstable, the more our home became broken. Mom started going out again, drinking even more than before. This time mom wasn't showing up for days, leaving us kids to fend for ourselves.

That's when I took on the mother role with my baby brother and sister. I always listened to mom and what she told me: keep the house clean, get Cassie and Craig to school, and do not mouth off to her, and never answer the door to anyone.

I was a full-blown mother to two children I couldn't stand at the time, sheesh lol. One day mom was missing in action. I was reaching out to my friends asking if they had any canned goods, I could grab to feed these kids. I wonder now why no one ever called children service on us?

One time she was gone for three days, and she showed up married to Steve. I was so pissed! This guy was gone from our house for a month this time round and as soon as they walked in married, he started his shit. He walked towards the kitchen cabinets opening them all and throwing the dishes he claimed wasn't washed enough, into the sink. This asshole would cuss us kids clean out, calling us every name in the bad book - we were children dick! But God forbid we ever say anything back at him - trust me we knew better to ever talk back. Growing up in a household back then, I dare you to sass off.

Child abuse was brushed under the rug. The more Steve messed up, the more I was the one who got the shit end of the deal. This is where I tell you how bad things got dealing with a mother with mental illness and drug addiction.

CHAPTER 7

"I CAN'T MAKE YOU LOVE ME" Bonnie Raitt

The marriage didn't make him a better man, as she hoped for. It just made him more of a monster, gave him a sense of full control. The consequences behind this madness were terrifying for us kids. The more mom went out, the more parties at the house we lived.

By that time, I was a worn soul. One night she decided to have one of her famous parties. At these parties was loud music, lots of drugs and alcohol, and don't let me leave out the weirdos.

Mom put a pool table in the living room and huge speakers where everyone laughed, drank, and smoked their reefer. No one ever brought their children over during these times, of course not, why would they? This one particular night, mom had some of the same faces over to the house as well as a few unfamiliar men.

They all wore black leather jackets and reeked of liquor. I had school in the morning, and I was fed up with the loud music and everyone's mouths. Covering my head with a pillow, after getting Cassie and Craig tucked in, I screamed with anguish hoping mom and her friends would leave. I wanted one night of rest; I was only a kid. I remember that night feeling very uneasy within myself.

The house got quiet, and I knew better than to walk downstairs to check on everything, so I fell asleep. I was startled by an unfamiliar face creeping into my bedroom. This was when I realized monsters under my bed were as real as you and I. He climbed into my bed covering my mouth from anyone hearing my cries. He forced his fist between my little legs, spreading them wide open, smelling like a bar. He rushed to get his pants down far enough to pull his penis out and pushing himself inside me. I remember throwing up, and the next thing I remember I was waking up from the alarm.

It was time to get the kids up for school. I sat up in pain holding on to my stomach. There was a puddle of blood I had to clean up before anyone saw it, but first let me get these kids off to school.

I remember Cassie pointing at the blood on my legs. I told her to mind her business. Once I got the two them sent to school, I knew mom wouldn't mind if I stayed back to clean her mess up. I tippy toed around her passed out body on the floor, lying face down. I knew better to wake her from a drunk night. I rushed to get rid of the bloody sheets, in hopes the beer cans would hide them.

I still couldn't comprehend what had happen to me, shit I didn't have time to think, let alone figure out what trauma was at that point of my life. I remembered the feeling I had when I drank my first Budweiser, so I grabbed one out the fridge and drank it. An hour later I consumed enough where I lost count.

CHAPTER 8

"TIL IT HAPPENS TO YOU" Lady Gaga

Mom woke up confused looking as always, finding me crying in a corner surrounded with beer cans. She yelled, "What the fuck are you doing home?" I looked up at this woman with tears falling from my face and I screamed back at her, "I was raped mom!" Her face went from being confused to becoming a worried mother, someone I haven't seen for quite some time. She helped me up and noticed I was a tad bit drunk. I sat down at the kitchen table while she rushed around looking for a clean rag. Once she got one, she sat down next to me and handed me a glass of water, told me to drink it up.

She looked at me and asked me what happened, promising me she wouldn't get upset with me. That statement alone had me confused. I was open to my mother for the first and last time that mid-afternoon. Instead of reassuring my safety or showing me warmth from a loving mother, I received a smack across the lips. That was the first time I had seen how horrifying the world could be.

I had seen how other children lived their lives, and I never understood why I was put into this one. Mom's mental state wasn't just waring on her, but also on myself. I would sneak and call my grandparents at night crying to them, telling them mom was drunk again. I would make them promise never to tell I called; they never did. My grandparents Max and Rita Cisco were the best people I have ever known.

They were Chris's parents, and they never looked at me like I wasn't one of their own. To be honest I was their favorite, and everyone knew it. By the time I was nine I was tortured in many ways, physically and mentally.

I was a full-time mother to my siblings and my mother's caretaker. I knew no matter how many times I was told by an adult never to talk about the horrifying events that I had endured as a child, I wasn't going to be able to keep their promises for much longer. My grandpa Max made a Cisco paddle as thick as a two by four. The last event before I let my heart spill to get help, was on a weekend that I went to my dad's. I loved my dad with my whole heart, but I knew there wasn't any guarantee I would be safe from my mother if I opened up to him.

CHAPTER 9

"WHEN DOVES CRY" Prince

My intuitive feeling was right. Chris called me over to his car to sit me down and started asking me questions about what was going on at home. I sat in silence listening to the promises. He said, he wouldn't be upset with me if I told him the truth.

I did however take the chance to tell my father what was happening, and he looked at me and asked me if I wanted to live with him. I told him yes and explained I just wanted to be a kid that was safe again. Chris's tears reassured me he meant what he had promised me. My dad said, "Crystal, I'm taking you back to grab all your belongings and brings you back home with me."

He did not know that he was going to be against a war with my mother. My mother wouldn't give up without a fight and she would feel betrayed. Chris did exactly what he promised.

He drove me back, and looked at me, telling me not to be scared. I do believe he was telling himself this. We walked into my mother's doors, and she asked, "What the fuck is going on?" He looked at me and told me to go to my room and start packing. I did that, listening to them yelling and screaming at one another. I rushed and was throwing what I could into a bag.

Cindy was screaming, "Chris, you're not taking her with you, she's staying here." Chris screaming back, "Yes I am taking her and there's nothing you can do about it". It went on for what felt hours, Chris asked her "How did you let this happen to my daughter?", and mom yelling back, "She's not your daughter, she's mine".

Cindy and Chris grabbing both my arms, I found myself back between a tug a war. Mom told him he would have to take her to court to get his hands on me and Chris screamed at her, "What the fuck happened to you Cindy?"

That day I watched the second man in my life walk out those doors without me.

CHAPTER 10

"DOWN WITH THE SICKENESS" Disturb

There I was stuck with mother dearest on fire. She grabbed my bag I had wrapped around my shoulder and neck, and ripped it off me, dragging me in the back room, grabbing that Cisco paddle.

I knew I was in deep shit. I started screaming, "Mom please don't hurt me." I begged for my life that day. I was picked up by my neck, slammed against the walls and once I fell to the ground gasping for air, she started beating me with that Cisco paddle. The more I moved, the more I got hit everywhere on my body. The last swing she took was against my back and elbow. It split in half.

I thank God that damn paddle was in pieces, even if it meant over my limp body. When she started walking out the room she said, "You want to act like you're grown and be on your own, I'm going to give you your wish bitch." She slammed the door behind her and all I could do was scoot my back against the wall in the corner of the room, watching and waiting for that door to reopen.

My arms were wrapped around my legs, and I rocked myself back and forth, praying to the sky. An hour went by, and mom came back into the room walking towards the closest. Throwing all my clothes on the floor and telling me I was getting out of her house, and that she never wanted to see me again. As scared as I was, I started picking up everything she threw down. I was nine years old, small built. The strength I was given by the universe that day was incredible. I got everything in my mom's trunk, walking passed Cassie and Craig, seeing the confusion and worry in their eyes-it brought the guilt of leaving them behind.

When I grabbed the last few things mom threw at me, I remembered them both sitting side by side, sad asking me not to leave them. It killed me inside. I told them, "I promise I'll be back for you." I cried all the way to my grandparents' house. When we pulled up, Cindy popped her trunk and told me to come get my shit, and if I dropped anything she'd be beating me all the way to that door. I begged God not to let me drop a thing. My prayers were answered, and I made it.

I looked behind me and watched my mom pull off. That moment I felt safe. That moment with tears of fear running down my face, I knew I would never go back to that woman.

CHAPTER 11

"I MISS THE DAYS" NF

With everything still in my arms, I opened the door my grandparents always left unlocked in case I needed to get in. That was one of the things they would both tell me on those late-night phone calls I made to them.

They were both at work, but I knew in my heart they wouldn't send me back. My grandma Rita walked in the door and saw me sitting on one of their stools with all my belongings I still had in my arms. I was still scared to let anything fall.

She ran to me crying, "Oh my God Crystal, are you ok?" She rushed around, grabbing my things out my arms, standing me up, lifting my shirt up and spinning me around. She saw the welts from the Cisco paddle - the horror of the abuse she saw with her own eyes were more devastating than the abuse I had been taking the past four years. Grandma fed me, and I remember she looked worried.

I asked her, "What's wrong grandma?" Grandma told me before I was allowed to live there, that it had to be okayed by my grandpa. Shortly my grandpa walked in, looking right at me, walked up and kissed me on my forehead. He sat down in his chair, lit his cigarette, and looked at both of us and asked, "Why is everyone so sad today?" My grandma looked at him in tears and said, "Max it happened again. I can't send her back to Cindy." He stood up and said, "Of course we aren't sending her back, she's home, where she belongs. "

My grandpa said, "Rita get some ideas on how you want to fix her room up." I ran in my grandpa's arms thanking him for saving my life. My grandma and I took my things to what turned into my bedroom for twelve years.

My dad came later that evening trying to share his opinion on the situation, and my grandpa simply said, "Chris she's not going back, this is her home and nothing you or Cindy could do or say can change this." That night my grandma made dinner, and when I tried to clean up the mess, she told me to sit down and that she could handle it.

I was shocked. I was able to just sit down. She started my shower and took me to the closet where she hung up all my cloths and picked out my outfit for school the next morning. I laid in bed that night with my night light on. My grandpa brought it for me. He knew I feared the dark without me ever telling him. My grandpa was the best man in my entire life.

I could not help but cry that night, wondering if Cassie and Craig were ok. That was the first time I had to choose myself. Leaving them behind broke my heart in places I didn't know I could hurt.

CHAPTER 12

"TIME AFTER TIME" Cyndi Lauper

I woke up the next morning with actual breakfast and lunch money. My grandpa took me to school, and I went looking for Craig and Cassie. When I saw them, I rushed to them, "Craig, Cassie," I yelled in a joyful voice. I saw them both look right at me, put their heads down and they kept walking. My heart felt sick- I ran behind some trees and threw up.

Years later I was told mom sat them both down and told them I wasn't their sister and not to speak to me or they would be in trouble. Even at the age of nine I knew that was wrong. But I didn't want them hurt, so I never said a word to them, and I just waited for them to come to me in hopes that they could forgive me for leaving them.

That year was the first year I was a kid again. I ran around with a smiling heart and joy in my soul. I finally had a home at 501 W. Kildare! I soaked up every bit of the love I was receiving from both grandparents. Everywhere they went, they took me with: from the flea markets they traveled to set up on their own, to the auctions my grandpa took me to on the weekends. I went to bed peacefully, and to school with a rested soul.

I got to play with my cousin and friends knowing there would not be any yelling from intoxicated parents. Grandma took me shopping for school clothes and supplies - something I never got before. Going to school with new clothes and shoes felt great. Once in a while I would yell, "I love you Craig, I love you Cassie," so they always knew I loved them!

Time went on and I started making friends. Grandma let me spend the night with them and let them stay at my house. I was experiencing a normal childhood and I adored it. I adored it so much I started taking advantage of my grandparents' love.

The first couple of years I was with them, I never heard the word no. Like any other kid did, I figured out how to use that to my advantage. My first friend was this little girl that talked back to her mother. I remember feeling horrible for her mom. This type of language towards adults was foreign to me, but I caught on quickly. I remember my grandma saying, "You're no longer allowed to hang out with Tiffany."

I was pissed, and I fought it as much as I could get away with. Soon, Tiffany's mom moved her away. Once again, I felt empty-every time I got close to someone, they seemed to leave.

CHAPTER 13

"WHAT ABOUT YOUR FRIENDS" TLC

I remember walking into my classroom noticing a little girl I knew from my previous schools. Her name was Lynn. Me and her instantly became best friends. She was rough and beautiful, and boy did she have a mouth on her. Lynn quickly introduced me to her sister Elizabeth, who was only a year older than Lynn, and four months younger than me. The three of us were inseparable. I remember we were underneath the playground equipment and Elizabeth and Lynn started cussing-I could not believe my ears. I looked at them and asked, "Are you allowed to cuss?"

They both laughed and told me yes. They said their mom let them cuss. Then they both looked at me "Aren't you allowed to cuss?"

I lied and told them of course I am. The sisters looked at one another, laughed loudly, turned, and looked at me and said, "Cuss then!"

I spoke up and said, "Fuck both of you." We all three laughed so hard, but I remember feeling like God was going to strike me dead right there at that instance. I felt so horrible for cussing. Looking back, I knew it was wrong, and I was watering myself down just to fit in.

I was twelve years old, and at this age I started getting into trouble. Between mouthing off to my grandparents I noticed girls flocked to me. I was a leader that had no clue how to lead at that moment in time. My leadership got myself and everyone around me into deep shit.

Elizabeth, Lynn, and I found a gas can in my grandpa's garage. We had heard stories about the other kids huffing gas, so we looked at one another and started huffing it. I can tell you now, I do not believe I was high, but it was a step towards years of self-destruction.

Elizabeth wasn't too big on huffing, but she loved her cigarettes and pot. My grandparents were always working, and everyone's parents either sold weed or smoked pot. Most of the Northside kids had parents for our plugs. Even when our parents didn't know it, they were our resource of getting high.

CHAPTER 14

"THIS IS WHAT MADE US GIRLS" Lana Del Ray

I smoked pot for the first time when I was twelve, behind my grandparents' house. Everything seemed quiet in my head, just like when I drank my first Budweiser. I started stealing cigarettes from my grandma's pack she left lying around, taking handfuls to Lynn and Elizabeth's house.

Around this same time, I made another best friend named Marie, another Northside girl. Her mom, and stepdad sold lots of pot, and we figured why not take a couple handfuls of it. With cigarettes and weed always on us, we became the popular girls-the girls, troubled boys wanted to be around.

 Us girls never dressed up girly - we wore our jeans past our butts and our oversized T-shirts tucked in the front and hung low in the back. I believe none of us girls wanted to show off our beauty too much due to the molestations that had happened in most our lives. My crew of girlfriends - well let's just say we had a lot in common.

We were all very beautiful, we were all messed with as children, and we were growing angrier by the minute. We were smart girls; we just didn't see it at the time. Between the trauma in our homes, and trying to fit in on the streets, none of us had time to think about our choices later in life.

Lynn, Elizabeth, and I were walking from my grandparents - we always cut through Rob Park, which was our stomping grounds. While we were cutting through the park to meet up with our other friends, I looked up and there was my mom and dick on the stick, playing tennis.

Lynn said "Look Crystal, there's your mom." I said, "Fuck her, just keep walking". My mom and I looked right at one another and never said a word to each other. My heart was no longer scared of that woman, but angry at her. I was thirteen.

We hit a couple of blocks and that's when we linked up with Marie- she became my greatest friend out of everyone. We would sit on her porch and waited until her mom left the house. We saw two Indian girls across the street yelling and screaming at each other. I asked, "Who are those girls?" She replied "The big one is Sky, and the little one is River."

Marie went on telling me how their mom would always let them do what they wanted, and how Sky would sleep with all types of grown men. I watched Sky cussing out her mother and River running after her two little puppies, looking irritated at both sister and mom. I told Marie to follow me across the street so I could talk to them.

CHAPTER 15

"FUCK THE WORLD" 2PAC

I walked up to River and Sky and asked them if they wanted to smoke the joint we were about to light up, after Marie's mom left the house. They both looked at one another and said "Yep, we sure do."

I told them we would be right back. We walked across the street waving goodbye to Marie's mother while she was getting into her car. As soon as we saw the car disappear down the road, we ran into the house straight to her parents' hiding spot. Unwrapping the foil that covered what I know now was a brick of weed, we snapped two handfuls off and stuck it in the purse I carried just for our drugs.

We quickly went back across the street, and I instantly tested the waters with their living situation. "Can we smoke this in the house?", I asked. Sky said "Hell yeah, we can my mom don't give a fuck what we do."

That house became our party house. I now had a crew of six, and everyone knew us. They knew not to fuck with us, and they knew we always had the best green on the Northside. When we all started going to North Middle school, it didn't take long to figure out that we were the most popular girls there. We fought anyone who looked cross-eyed at us, girls or boys, we didn't discriminate. Most of us got suspended from school, or just skipped the days we felt like skipping. We had our own table in the cafeteria, and everyone knew not to sit there no matter if we showed up for school or not.

On this day we were all there. Imagine this cafeteria as a jungle full of misunderstood children thinking we knew everything about life, at least 300 at a time. All of us girls were at our table cracking jokes. Suddenly, I saw this girl with a tray of food in her hands walk right up to a schoolmate and say, "Talk shit now bitch."

The girl she called a bitch stood up and before you knew it Gelly took her tray and cracked it over her head. I sat and watched security drag her out of school. We had first period together, so when she came back to school after being suspended, I asked her if she wanted to come over for a slumber party I was throwing while my grandparents were leaving town that coming weekend. She said, "Hell yeah,"

I asked if she could get beer? She said she could try, and I told her "Don't try just do it."

That following Friday she came up to me and told me she's been scooping out a nearby drive-through in our neighborhood, and that every morning there was a beer truck that pulled in the back to unload. I gathered my crew and we left after first period. We had a plan to jump into the beer truck and have an assembly line outside the beer truck while two of us handed them cases of 40'oz's, and that's what we did. We were so quick the guy driving the truck never knew what hit him. We hid our cases of beer behind my back yard, and when my grandparents drove off, I called everyone over. Before they left the house, I snuck the keys to my aunt's corvette to surprise my friends with a stolen car. Yes, I was a bad influence and very troubled as we all were.

At this point of our lives, we lived on the edge not knowing what was going to become of any of our souls. I just knew I wanted to feel needed and fit in with the best of them. Everyone showed up, and we started pulling out the weed and alcohol. Next thing I knew we were all crying about everything we all been through. Gelly was nicknamed that night, because she was the first to cry about what happened to her as a young girl. I wanted to make us all happy, so I pulled out the keys to the corvette and said, "Come on, let's all go take a ride."

We climbed into the car and turned the stereo as loud as it could go and sped off. We were so lucky we didn't get hurt. I think about everything we did for a rush and sheesh…. blessed is the word that protected us all.

CHAPTER 16

"DON'T LET ME BE MISUNDERSTOOD" The Animals

When I ponder on the influence I was, I can't help but feel somewhat responsible for leading a group of girls down such a dark path. I was the kid everyone's parents wanted their children to stay away from. At the time I never understood why I wasn't invited to normal birthday parties or sleep overs. After having my own children, I totally understood the fear a parent would have that protected their own child. I was a lost soul at a very young age, and I had no clue about life. I was raised within a party, watching my parents and their friends laugh and have fun…...at least that is what I thought fun was about.

 To my readers, if any of you are my childhood friends, I want to apologize for not knowing better. I want all of you to know you were a huge part of my survival and muse to become a better person, and a better friend. I will always love you Northside girls until the world blows! I would not have been able to get through such a dark place at that time of my life, if I did not have you as one of my friends so, thank you, to each and every one of you beautiful souls. I love you!

We grew up quickly and most of us had already seen the devil himself, through what we wanted to believe was an angel.

My heart is full of pain when I think back of not just the rough times we all endured, but how we all made it through it, alone later in life. I am very proud of us all, no matter where some of you are at in life. I will never give up faith for you.

Growing up fast meant meeting fast boys, and when I mean fast, I mean boys who were running the streets, committing crimes, and screaming fuck the world! I will speak for myself; I absolutely loved the idea of a bad boy. As uncomfortable as I was being a girl in a man's world, I embraced it.

When I saw a couple of my friends already having boyfriends, I can't lie, I thought it was sickening. Elizabeth took on such a mother role in her household, I guess she felt like it was time to settle down, quickly too…. sheesh. Lynn and I would watch her sister get ready to go to high school parties while we sat on the couch watching our favorite movie *Cry Baby*. Elizabeth would make fun of us for acting our age. Looking back at these moments I know even though Lynn and I didn't attend these high school parties, we still were lost souls trying to hang on to the innocence we still had.

CHAPTER 17

"KING CRY-BABY" Johnny Depp

Lynn would cry to her sister, begging her to stay home. She was always worried about Elizabeth getting hurt by a weird guy, but Elizabeth gave no fucks and left us in the dust. One day Elizabeth didn't feel good, so her mom took her to the urgent care. Lynn went along. The doctor came in after examining her and told her she wasn't sick, she was pregnant.

Her mother was pissed, and lord when you pissed their mom off, it was like a bomb dropping into a village. They drove off and Elizabeth was in the back crying and Lynn was upfront trying to eat, when their mother back handed Lynn in the mouth. All Lynn could do was hold her mouth that was filling up with blood and ask why she was the one who got hit?

We were twelve and thirteen when this all happened - talking about a fast lifestyle we all lived in…. sheesh. As little girls, we had no clue what the fuck was going on in the world, nor were we aware of what the world was going to bring to us just by the way we were living.

Elizabeth's belly grew quickly and as children we thought it was cute. What we were not aware of, is it was cute to play dolls, not barring children as a child, but my question is still, who do we have to blame for these thoughts? We were angry children growing into angry adolescents.

We had to stick up for one another. The motto was, 'if your sibling came home beat up, you were getting beat up.' For me, I would rather get kicked out of school and take a suspension than come home and get beaten by one of my parents for not sticking up for a sibling or friend.

CHAPTER 18

"GIMME SHELTER" Rolling Stones

Every holiday my dad Chris would yell for me out front my grandparents' house, and every holiday my mom had me in a dress I despised. I would walk outside and behind me was my grandma saying to my dad, "Chris she's a girl, don't have her do this."

All that did was pump him up even more to have me in my dress, beating up my brother and male cousins. I never wanted to hurt my brother though. I was his protector, not someone that should have been hurting him, so I hated it. But my dad and uncle would scream, "Get him Crystal."

At first, I wouldn't move, then my dad would push Craig into me so hard I had no choice but to push him back.

Craig being my dad's only son at the time, I'm sure felt like he had to show off, so Craig would instantly start swinging on me, and all I could do is lose my shit on that kid. Every time it ended up with Craig crying. My dad would have to peel me off him, and by the time I was pulled off my little brother, I was in a full black out-waking up from a force of anger had me in tears.

I would run off behind the closest woods I could find to hide from what I was taught was weak: God forbid you ever cry in front of Dad. I would sit in those woods and cry with guilt in my heart for ever hurting him. I understand that at the time it was just for entertainment, but in my heart, I hated every bit of it.

CHAPTER 19

"SCHOOL'S OUT" Pink Floyd

Elizabeth was pregnant: we were twelve and thirteen and in middle school. Elizabeth was big and pregnant at the time, and I was walking in line with my class down the hallway. I looked over and I saw her standing in the office crying. I stepped out of line hearing my teacher yelling my name to get back in line. As usual I did not pay attention to anything she was trying to tell me and walked into the office where Elizabeth stood crying.

I asked her, "Why the fuck are you crying?"She looked at me and said she told her teacher she needed to use the bathroom; due to the pregnancy, the baby was always sitting on her bladder. This made her always needing to use the restroom. Once again, we had no clue about pregnancies. The teacher did though, and making someone I considered my sister sit in pain holding her urine made me furious.

I grabbed her hand and said "Go to the bathroom now. "Our principal at the time had a stuttering problem and tried getting words out his mouth that he forbade Elizabeth to use the restroom.

At first Elizabeth was worried to walk to the bathroom, but I reassured her she was going, and she was safe to go. Long story short, I got into big trouble sticking up for her and got expelled. If you had asked me if I cared back then, I would have told you no. If you would ask me today if I would have changed that choice I made, I would tell you no. I stood up for what I believed in, in many ways.

Even though I was a lost child, I still had a heart of gold and no matter who you were, if I was around, nothing bad would happen to you. On the other hand, yes, I could have handled it somewhat better. No regrets, I learned this throughout my darkest of times.

CHAPTER 20

"FIGHT FOR YOUR RIGHTS" Beastie Boys

I was put on probation, which started from the age of twelve to my late 30's. I always found myself on some type of probation. Probation officers were my parents- as much as I did not see it at the time, I'm grateful. I thank God daily they were a part of my growth. They never held punches, and they had no issue throwing my butt behind bars when I needed the time out. They were more than discipline; they were my role models.

I was an angry kid and growing to become an angrier adult. They saw something in me that I could not. I pissed them off regularly, not understanding at the time the possibilities I held in my life. One thing was certain: they never gave up on me. I love and adore what they gave me: stability!

See, growing up I didn't have someone telling me I had to go to school, or how important school was, or how it was ok to become successful. Nor did I know it was ok to forgive my mother and understand that she DID HER BEST! If anyone of my old probation officers is reading this: Thank You. Thank you for caring enough for a lost angry kid that was creating destruction for a life. Thank you for guiding and leading me to a better way of life, and even when you didn't know if I was listening. Trust my words in the book I am writing-I heard every word.

CHAPTER 21

"SUPERMAN" Eminem

Clark was the first boy I loved. I am however very aware it was puppy love. At the time, there wasn't a soul that could tell me any different. Clark was the cutest thing I laid my eyes on. He had sandy blonde hair with freckles and the brightest blue eyes I'd ever seen. I was in love and my heart needed him in my life. Just like the movie superman, he was my Clark, and I was in hopes of being his Lois.

In Crystal-land I truly believed he was the superman that came to save me from every bit of pain the world had served me on a platter. I was fourteen, in middle school, and I watched this boy walk around with no fear in his heart. He smoked cigarettes and hung with a crew that was ten times worse than mine.

To me he was the missing part I yearned for. This kid was in my first period class every semester and he smelled so good. I remember how well dressed he always stayed. He was the beginning of my heart aches, and I knew it, but didn't want anything more but to have him in my life. A walking disaster with eyes of an angel, I knew he was troubled. I knew in my heart I could change him, and we would live happily ever after. Yeah, I know, what an imagination right?

I started making my friends to go with me to the places I knew he and his friends would be. Looking back, we were walking into the lion's den and didn't know it…or did we? After showing up everywhere, we finally I got noticed by them. To be quite honest, we were noticed everywhere we went. This brought a lot of the hell that ended up part of our lives.

Clark and I started hanging out tight. We started off as friends, but the more I stuck around the more I realized that I wanted more from him. I would try hooking him up with a couple of my friends before I ever told him I was the one who wanted to be with him.

Clark and I would run the streets and I would be the lookout guy when he was doing something illegal. I always hated being the lookout guy. I wanted to be involved in anything Clark was involved in. I gave him lots of credit today that I'm sure he has no clue of. He protected me from anything that he felt that would harm me. Outside of breaking my heart into pieces. I stayed with this same kid for twenty some odd years, off and on-more off than on. We have two daughters together and two grandchildren now. We did get married, and we lived in a beautiful home he redid himself.

CHAPTER 22

"25 TO LIFE" Eminem

By that time in our lives, I had pure hate for this guy. Backing up some years before the madness, we were running the streets of Lima, Ohio with our friend Jacob. It was winter and the snow came to our waist, we didn't mind it, we loved the snow. Outside it hurt Clarks eyes from his eyes being so blue. We traveled to the quarries - there were stones like mountains surrounding a body of water.

Dangerous wasn't the word, but anything for a thrill, we took it on. To us the quarries were a place to be free during the hot summer days. Hit most of us did not have the money to get in the pools, so we would gather up as a group and head to the quarries jumping off the highest stone there was. We all heard the stories that there were tunnels that could suck us under if we would get close to any of them, and the stories were true. Luckily, we were protected souls from the stars above because no one I hung with ever got hurt, but many kids I didn't know, did.

Clark, Jacob, and I thought it would be cool to ice skate at the quarries - it was a very stupid idea. We had to climb down a tall mountain of stone to get to the body of water that was frozen. The closer we got, the more I started thinking we should turn around: my gut was warning me. Once we got down to the frozen water, I saw it in all three of our eyes. We needed to rethink this bright idea. Instead, Clark yelled, "Jacob, get your fat ass on that ice."

Jacob was the biggest one and if it held him, it sure in the hell would hold us. Jacob told Clark to fuck off, so Clark's crazy ass went walking onto the ice one foot at a time, slowly sliding across the ice holding on to a limb from a tree that had fallen onto the ice. Next thing I knew, I heard the ice breaking around Clark, and I started screaming, "Get off the ice, it's breaking!"

Clark looked back at me and all I saw was the ice under his feet shattering. Clark fell in the water and Jacob ran after him without a second thought and grabbed his little ass out that water so quickly, I couldn't believe my eyes.

Clark didn't die that day due to Jacob saving him. Jacob was one of our greatest friends growing up, a true solid guy from when we were kids till audlts. We were all worn out from all the excitement, so Jacob told us he was walking home. Clark looked at me and asked me to walk him home…yeah, me walk him home, what the fuck.

And of course, I did. That day was our first kiss. I was so happy. We walked all the way to Union St. We made it to the ally of his house standing in snow that was never ploughed, and I remember looking down at Clark. I was taller than him, and he got on his tippy toes and kissed me. I walked home alone that day with a smile from ear to ear. I finally got the boy of my dreams. Not knowing shit about life, I know now that situation was a beautiful disaster, and I speak this way because Clark and I came from broken homes and went through a lot of the same abusive atmosphere, sexually.

CHPATER 23

"LOVE THE WAY YOU LIE" (PART 2) Eminem

His mother was a single mom who raised her children with love, and protected them with all her might. I will state sometime, no matter how much of a protector you might think you are, you cannot live a life of partying and think your children will be safe.

I watched this woman be the best mother in the world and still live with the guilt she held from not protecting her youngest from a monster who took his innocence. In his early youth this caused Clark to reach out to anything that numbed his mind from racing or going back to those memories he kept even from me, for years.

At the age of fifteen, I found out that I was pregnant. By that time in our relationship, Clark was very controlling. He monitored who I spoke to and where I went. It was so toxic that we ended up being known as the couple who fought all the time. I must be honest, us fighting the way we did - I thought was normal. I manifested a partner that I adored, who came from the same type of lifestyle I did.

I remember I could not wait to have a boyfriend I could fight with. That's how naïve I was at such a young age. Watching my parents fight with one another was the norm for me. When Clark started hitting me and making me feel worthless, I knew this could not be a healthy relationship. I just knew in my heart that love had to be more than what we have learned from others.

I started coming home with his handprints around my arms. It got so bad, I started to wear long sleeve shirts. This was so I didn't have to answer any more questions to the ones asking if Clark was hitting me. You learn from observation. Watching my mother make up lies to protect the man that was beating her, was instilled in my mind as the right thing to do.

Even though I thought that way, I still held on to the hopes that always stuck with me: "there was more to life than this shit."

I was six months pregnant when Clark climbed on top of me for the last time. I allowed him to hit on me. I remember my belly so big at six months, and I remember every time I went to the doctor's office hearing her heartbeat, how much I fell in love with this little human I have not met yet. I promised to her and myself, I would never let anyone hurt her the way they did her mom and father.

Clark got on top of me, and I took him by surprise and beat his little ass up and down his mother's house that day. I called my grandpa and told him to come get me because I just beat Clark up. In 1.5 seconds, my grandpa was there to pick me up. All I could think about was my baby being hurt, and all I knew was fight and flight, which I got good at doing, unfortunately.

CHAPTER 24

"RUN" Pink

After giving birth to our daughter Corie, his mother wanted DNA testing. I had no concerns about the outcome, 99.9% Clark was the doner. My life was an upside-down spiral of confusion.

At the age of sixteen I was now a mother to a little girl who came out looking just like me: 6pounds 14oz's 18inch long, she was perfect. I know all mothers state that their child came out perfect, but I mean it. Corie was perfectly round: a head full of black wavy hair and eye lashes for days. Corie's hair was so full and so long it came past her earlobes.

She never cried and she slept through the night from day one. She was such a good baby. I would cry thinking something was wrong because she just never cried. I know now why - she was preparing her lungs for the day she found her voice, and lord knows those lungs made up for being the best baby. I named her after all my best friends at the time…Yeah, I know, but I was still a little girl myself, poor kid. Corie, Elizabeth, Lynn, Marie. My greatest creation my biggest blessing from the stars above! This little girl saved my life.

When I pushed this little girl out on May 25th, 1996, I felt what true love felt like. My mother stood there with me when I pushed her out and she started screaming to everyone, "She looks just like her mother!" She wasn't bull shitting. She was my twin I manifested!

I remember being a little girl wondering why I did not look like anyone that I was related to. I had black frizzy long hair with amber eyes, and my skin was so dark my knees would look dirty. Everyone around me was pale skinned, blue or green eyes and blonde straight hair. I wished to the stars every night I went to bed as a little girl, that I had one person in this world I looked like. This is how my beautiful daughter Corie came into my life.

The moment this little beauty was born I no longer felt alone in this life I was living. I was a sixteen-year-old mother, living with my grandparents. Jumping back - when I was 8 months pregnant, everyone in my family warned me that out of everyone my grandpa would be the most disappointed and what I was told, disown me. I stand here speaking highly of the best man in my whole life. My grandpa Max Cisco was the only one who did not treat me poorly during this time in my life. On Mother's Day in 1996, my grandpa took all the women in our family out to a Mother's Day dinner that evening.

I was sitting in the family room big and pregnant, depressed, and sad that I was not invited due to the shame I brought to the family for being pregnant. Everyone was gathering into my grandfather's van walking out the house, and I heard the door shut. I looked up and grandpa was standing in front of the doorway, motioning me to come over. I got up seeing one hand behind his back, walking towards him.

 He swung his arm from behind and presented a flower saying, "Happy Mother's Day Sweetie."

One of the most loving memories. I knew right there, that even if no one in the world believed I was capable of becoming a good mother, that man's faith and prayers made it happen for Corie and me today.

CHAPYER 25

"MOCKINGBIRD" Eminem

Writing this book, I have pondered on how much I should allow my readers to know. Getting the truth out started to be the biggest reason to write this book. Then something happened this past weekend and I could not believe the current wave that changed the game: my son!

Although the truth will run through this book like a magical riverside on a beautiful spring day, for my children's peace of mind, there are some things we keep close to our hearts and privately in the dark part of each one of our souls.

One of the greatest lessons in life I have learned is: less is best. Yes, the truth will always set you free, but love conquers all! So even when your life has been full of pain and heart ache, we were all blessed with something oh so beautiful: our hearts.

With that being said, my children are my heart. I birthed three, and when I gave birth to these legendary humans, their powers grew so beautifully that they were able to cut this old lady's soul into three parts of the rising sun each morning!

Corie was my first born, so she holds the trophy of being my first love. With this trophy she became a hero of her mother's life. With every breath I took after delivering her, I promised I would live for her, teaching her right from wrong, even at our hardest of times. I've made damn sure she understood the madness behind every choice we make throughout our lives. The love I hold for this beauty runs so deep.

Corie never knew what crawling was. She went from being held in her mother's arms to walking. I was in total bliss and obsessed with this little human I made. Putting her down was not an option. When she was fourteen, she looked at me with tears in her eyes and asked me to take her off her pedestal. I had to step back for a second and think before I said another word. We were fighting that day. I stood back to wonder why my baby felt this way.

I looked into her eyes, and I told her, "Corie Elizabeth that pedestal is yours, and I will never take you down from that cloud."

I knew life started hurting my baby that day, I knew she was an empathic soul. I had to be careful what type of words I spoke, so she always understood her mother's love. I became a mother way before my time ,and many years of raising my siblings and guiding my parents, I learned a lot.

Today people will wonder if I have any regrets. I stand tall today with a heart full of joy to tell you I sure fucking do. But see, the regret I have, no longer rents a space in my soul. I look at life with a new set of eyes, and that alone feeds my mind with beauty and peace.

The day I took that pregnancy test and I saw two lines; my eyes opened my third eye. Corie has been her mother's saving grace! The soul that conquered all the beauty in every disaster. That's when I came up with my title in my life, "She Seen an Angel in Every Devil". So even though her father and I did not work out and yes, we went through hell trying to keep it together even at a young age, today I respect that man's devil.

Clark loved me as much as he allowed himself to love at that point of his life. Confused as I was, he was going through hell himself. He grew up in his own world, before me and became addicted to the substance of pain and suffering. And like all addicts, it's the lifestyle we learned to live in, that became comfortable. I call it an evil blanket. It took over Clark's life to the point he had no control. He became a mess, and he failed his responsibilities with his daughter.

CHAPTER 26

"SIMPLE MAN" Lynyrd Skynyrd

The year of 2001, I was twenty-one and I gave birth to my only son. That year was the year the world smacked me down. Adrian my son, was born March 21st, 2001, 7pounds 2 ounces and 21 inches long. The only man who took my heart and never gave it back. Mommy's Boogie. This is where my life starts jumping around, only the real will keep up!

Adrian's father was sentenced to four years in prison. I did not want to run back to my grandparents again, so here's how Clark and Lyfe intertwined, and became the fathers of my children. Lyfe became the love I had no clue existed, my biggest lesson and my worst heart break. To me, this man was my moon- nothing shined brighter than the moon in my life. When I became pregnant with our son, two months later, Lyfe was heading to do his bid behind bars. He became the 3rd man to walk out my life.

Not knowing the right thing to do, I ran back to Clark. I knew I broke that bond, and I take my own responsibilities due to that relationship. I was young and dumb and trying to survive with two small children.

Lyfe went to prison and Clark still loved me enough to accepts my son with open arms. That gave me the option to try and make things work one last time, before letting go for good. I found out about Clark's habits very quickly, I also found out after going to my 6 weeks checkup, I was once again pregnant.

My son was 3 months old, and my daughter had just turned 5. I could not believe my ears. Everything at that moment sounded like Charlie Brown's teacher. My ears were ringing while my doctor. went on explaining my options. With one child in a car seat and the other sitting there stating, "Mom is that another baby in your belly?"

Holy shit, I was in total disbelief. "How the fuck did this happen, why would he do this to me, how am I going to do this", said every emotion all at once. I had one in prison for drugs and one on drugs, two children, my sanity, and every fear hit me with a ton of bricks. I felt my body shutting down. I also felt my mind losing sight of reality.

My mother needed a place to stay, so of course I opened my door to her. The first week I let her in my home, I ran to her for advice in hopes she could finally guide me through this time in my life. I ran to every woman I looked up to in my life at that time. My mother told me to give the baby up for adoption. "Crystal Gail, you can't afford another child."

I ran to Clark's mother, crying and begging her to help me. She stated that she would not help me raise this child. I looked at her with disbelief. I told her I needed her to take the child for a little bit. I tried explaining my mental state needed to heal from every bit of trauma I've been through. She looked me in my eyes and said, "Crystal as mothers we have to make choices in life that doesn't feel good."

She went on to tell me, I had to decide if I was going to take on another child. That day was grey - there was not a light in the sky that shined, as if the universe just knew this would change my entire life.

CHAPTER 27

"ONE" Metallica

It poured down with rain just like the tears did down my cheeks, with pure misery and sadness. I made the decision on giving my little girl up for adoption. That week I went to my cousin's house where I went every weekend. I told her what was going on in my life and she guided me through the adoption process, but behind my back she spoke badly about me. This was when I realized everyone I was associated with, wasn't rooting me on in hopes I would lose in life.

I gathered my thoughts and saved enough money for a one-bedroom home for my children and I. I got a third shift job, started Corie in Kindergarten, and held on to my sanity as long as I could. I never begged so hard to people in all my life, until that year. I could not believe that I was surrounded by so many monsters who hid underneath my bed.

March 29th, 2002, was the day I gave birth to my daughter Emma. She came out 8 pounds 2 ounces and 19 inches long. She was a beautiful little girl; her skin was rosy, and her hair was sandy blonde. She was perfect, and as much as I tried hiding my feelings during my pregnancy, I could not hold on any longer when it was time to push this little beauty out.

I wrote her a letter the night before, and I tried to explain how much she meant to me. I told her there would not be a day that went by that I would not think of her. Today I still stand on these words. 20 years later, I stand tall with a missing link still to my heart.

"Emma, mommy loves you, and out of everything I've ever done in my life, there was never a moment I did not think of you or see you in my dreams."

I carried this beautiful soul for 9 months. I felt her first movement in life, and as the doctor. and nurses were running into the delivery room telling me to get ready to push her out, I grabbed a hold of my heart, and I fucking screamed!!! I screamed out the seconds I had left with her, and I screamed of the pain I was about to endure giving her away! The agonies of life were landing on my soul like bombs from a war. Everything flashed before my eyes: my sister Cassie standing next me holding my hand through it all, looking me in my eyes and telling me, "You got this sis."

I spoke back and with the very first time she heard me say, "I can't do this Cassie Jo." I lost my shit that moment. I held on long enough to give this baby life and held her for the first and last time in my life.

That day I died inside. That day I had my first nervous breakdown. I walked out of that hospital without my baby in my arms and I ran into my darkest of times - with a sword in one hand and my heart in the other, slaying every soul that came close to me.

I had two little children at home waiting for me. I could not let them see the pain in my now dark soul. I had to do everything I could not to ponder on what just happened to me. I was now part of the living dead. Trying to be a good parent to the humans I created, without a helping hand was the hardest job I have ever had. I was still in love with Lyfe and felt abandoned by Clark, and our families. I just remember standing in time spinning so fast I had no time to think about what I was doing wrong as a mother, a sister, a daughter, and #1 MYSELF. That is when I walked into, 'The House of The Rising Sun.'

CHAPTER 28

"THE HOUSE OF THE RISING SUN"

Every weekend I found myself suffering from the bottle of poison I washed down with every pill I threw back in hopes of swallowing my traumatic life. I knew I took on my parents' habits - inhaling anything that would put my mind at ease. Snorting the white powder as if I was floating on a cloud of unforgiveness. Washing my sins down with every sip of anger I held onto. With no empathy for male kind, I become the beast everyone asked for.

The men I had in my life were no longer something shiny and new and something pretty I loved looking at. Instead, I looked at them as sin and pure hate. I was so broken from what I chose to do-I blamed them for everything. I wanted them to suffer as much as I was suffering! When people were around, I put on a painful smile that lit up every room I walked into.

I remember thinking if I can't beat them, join them and take their souls. I walked around my home looking at the empty walls and filled every wall with pictures of Emma. Every weekend I was at a local bar, drinking until I could no longer lift my head. Snorting cocaine to wake up long enough to drive home and party until I heard those birds chirping. I bawled my eyes out every morning because I was still alive in a world full of darkness, so I grabbed my bottle of Xanax and threw back ten pills in hopes I could get through another day without anyone noticing my self-destruction.

Lyfe got out of prison and Clark left town. I moved in with my sister, her son, and my brother, who all needed a place to go to. We all watched my mother go down a deeper ditch with a guy that received three hundred blue football Xanax in the mail from the V.A. Life was insane, and at this point I was going with the flow. I remembered watching Lyfe sell drugs and making thousands. All I could think about was raising these children and making sure my siblings graduated. So, after linking up with Lima's drug dealers for my own use, I decided to use what I had to get a good deal on an ounce of cocaine. I can't lie I was worried I would turn out like the other girls and sell my soul. With that being said, I turned the game all the way around. I told myself I no longer lived in a man's world, that this world was mine. I was beautiful, smart, and I knew the ins and outs of the street law.

I was making money the only way I knew how, and I was going to make these sons of bitches respect me. Becoming a bitch was easy after everything I had been through. I used that to become a cold-hearted snake.

CHAPTER 29

"THUNDERSTRUCK" AC/DC

I started with an ounce of cocaine not worrying about the consequences from the LPD, or anyone around me including my children. I had seen how easy it was selling this shit and I saw how much everyone loved it. I couldn't believe how much money I was making or how much fun I was having doing it.

It was the first time I was finally doing what Crystal wanted to do, whatever the fuck I wanted. I no longer cared what a mother fucker was thinking of me, and I walked around like I ran shit. I did run shit. I noticed the guys flocked to my aid and wants. I had the whole world in my hands. I drove the nicest cars and dressed my children in the best clothes. You name it, they had it. I ran around from dusk till dawn, never seeing what the absence of being a mother was doing to Corie and Adrian. By that time, I had all my friends snorting this poison right along with me. Misery loves company and I was one miserable soul, without a conscious.

The fun started fading away after a couple years. The men I fed a dream of being my one and only. I was fed up with my shit, and I was growing tired. My runners were stealing from me and the men I would have around, were only around for the party.

No matter how much I was able to support my family from this income, it was not making me happy. I started falling out slowly. Having six ounces at a time hidden in my attic, my kids missing school and every question I had to answer with a lie, finally was coming to an end. I even had my mom standing by my side for the first time.

At first, I thought this life was bringing me all my desires, money, and my mother. I felt like as long as I fed her the drug, I could keep a close eye on her. She was such a free spirit, which was a job alone. I couldn't keep up any longer.

The man I had in my life looked at me one night and said to me, "Crystal, I love you and I need to speak to you, this isn't your life." I remember telling him I would come pick him up and we would have our last party together. I was so tired that night, I remember wanting to get up and get ready to go meet up with him. I fell asleep, I was so worn out. I woke up with my phone ringing off the hook. I answered it, and it was a mutual friend of him and me. He said, "Crystal, what are you doing?" I spoke up asking him what the fuck he thought I was doing. He quickly told me if I was not sitting down, I needed to. I sat up quickly asking him what's wrong.

"Crystal Jesse died".

CHAPTER 30

"FREE BIRD" Lynyrd Skynyrd

I could not believe my ears. I told him he was lying to me! He said, "I'm sorry Crystal he's gone." I dropped my phone and fell to my knee's crying uncontrollably. I could not believe he was gone. I could not comprehend that I had just lost one of my greatest friends.

That was the 5th man who walked out of my life. He was also the man that walked side by side with me – with every step of hell I walked into with his head held high, and his fist ready to knock out anyone who dared to steal from me or come at me to harm me. Jesse was a straight up solid man - that night I was supposed to be with him, that night cocaine took his life. I often wondered if it would have taken mine if I had shown up.

I was in my mid 20's thinking if I taught my children the total opposite of how I was raised. I did not trust anyone with either of my children. The thought of someone hurting them made me homicidal, so keeping them close to me was the only way they lived. I did not know I had to change. I blamed everyone but myself.

I became a victim and held on to the title for way to long. Feeling sorry for myself came easy and blaming the world came naturally. I knew something had to change; I just wasn't sure what yet.

Lyfe helped with the kids here and there, but he was too busy selling drugs and selling women. He would say he did not have time to baby sit. I never understood those words coming out a parent's mouth who helped make the child. Lyfe ended up getting busted again - this time it was fed time, and before he went in, he wanted my help on a plan he had, to help me and my friends. He knew I was selling drugs and to me, I thought he was just trying to make life easier on me. Boy was I wrong.

CHAPTER 31

"BLUE JEANS" Lana Del Rey

Every scam that man ever got me involved in, he would turn around and not only tell the police it was all me, but give them a map to my house to come pick me up. That is how much respect that man had for me. No respect whatsoever, but at that point of my life, I still saw an angel in his devil.

He was the one man I truly cared for. He was the man who taught me to be a woman in a good way and bad way. I remember the first time we made love and I was so happy but still shy, and I waited for him to say something. When he did, he turned to me and said," You know with all that great pussy you have, you should be selling it." Talk about a disappointment. I thought at the time he was so smart - he never cussed, and he was nice to me. One of the hardest things I've had to learn was to paint a picture of a narcist.

Lyfe was five years older than me, which made him the first older man I gave myself too. My home girls were going to a party that night, but I wanted to be alone, so I stayed home. Marie, River and Sky all went to a party with my cousin. The next morning, I was woken up by being told that the guy who owned the home was my type, whatever that meant. I found out it belonged to Lyfe and my chics were acting up not caring about life.

That was how all us girls lived so I can imagine what they were screaming. It makes me laugh every time I think about it! But they all got kicked out for disrespecting Lyfe's house and came home talking about me needing to meet this guy, and we would be perfect together. So, I hit my cousin up, telling him to link us all up one night. My cousin was hesitant about introducing me to Lyfe. I know now why he was - he wanted to protect me from what would end up happening in the near future.

I talked my girls into coming with me that night. My cousin drove Lyfe's Cadillac to come swoop us up. Lyfe wasn't in the car when it arrived. I found out that we had to drive and pick him up at another girl's apartment. Red flags were flying from the very jump, and every time I pushed them out my view.

CHAPTER 32

"FUCK FACES" Scarface

When he stepped into the car, Sky sat between us, and I remember both of us leaning forward to get a good look at each other. I thought to myself, "I wonder what the big deal is." The way my friends spoke I thought I would be looking at a God!

He was staring into my soul smirking; I knew I was in trouble, and I liked every bit of feeling out of control with this man. I was 17, and still had no clue about life.

Lyfe being wiser than me at the time, scared the shit out of me at first, so I did what I knew best, and I ran as many times as I could until I gave in to him. He was smart and had big dreams. He had a beautiful home and he kept lots of money in his pockets. Everyone who surrounded Lyfe, looked up to him and treated him like a boss. That made it easy for my curiosity to grow and stick around.

Lyfe started taking me to 5-star restaurants and on wild shopping sprees. He showed me what to wear and what looked good on my body. I was still just a girl wearing baggie jeans, T-shirts and my tennis shoes. Putting on fitted clothes and looking at what my parents created was a shocker.

I turned 18 and got my first apartment. My grandma did not want me taking Corie to my apartment, and at the time I did not understand. Being an older woman, I now understand my grandma was just looking out for Corie's best interests. The more I was involved with Lyfe, the less I was a mother, and as bad as I hate remembering my flaws as a mother, it was the truth. I thank the stars above we had two great grandparents.

Lyfe never cursed at me. He taught me how to bend my legs when I had on shorts or a dress, and he was the first man I fell head over heels for. He taught me without making fun of my lack of knowledge - he was the calm before the storm. I melted with every touch. I forgot everything that ever happened to me and I lost myself underneath that man, and felt safe doing it. With every kiss and every touch, I felt my soul crushing like the waves in an ocean. I loved him and I was in trouble for it.

CHAPTER 33

"EX-FACTOR" Lauryn Hill

One night he asked me where my parents were from, since we both were half white and half Hispanic. A question I never spoke about, since I never knew who my real father was, was what Cindy told me.

I honestly never wanted to reminisce about what broke up my family. Plus, who wants to talk about their mother not knowing who she slept with? To me Chris was my father, and no one deserved that title but that man. But Lyfe spoke to me with a calming voice, and it was always easy to open up to him. I was short with him at first and told him my mother was from Lima, Ohio and my dad from Toledo, Ohio.

He said, "Cool my people are from Toledo as well." We never spoke much more about it until 6 months later. I always knew how to steer away from that embarrassing situation. Lyfe wanted me to come over one night so he could cook for me and surprise me with the biggest reflection of my life. I came over, and after eating we snuggled up in bed. While lying in his arms Lyfe grabbed my chin, turned my face towards his and told me he loved me. I closed my eyes and I whispered back, "I love you too."

Seconds later both of our lives changed. He was kissing me and looking into my eyes and asked me, "Didn't you tell me your dad is from Toledo?"

I replied, "Yeah, why are you asking me?" He asked me his name and went on talking about his dad and family all from being there. Maybe they knew him? I sat up quickly knowing this conversation was going to be hard to talk about. I turned to him and said, "Lyfe, my mom had a one-night stand with some guy she was working with at Marko's Pizza, and she told me his nickname, but I rather not say it because it's embarrassing.

He grabbed my hands, calmed me and told me I could tell him anything. He promised to never laugh at me. I put my head down and said, "His name is Naco." Before I could look up Lyfe jumped out the bed and started pacing the room. Looking down with his head in his hands yelling "This can't be true!" I pulled the blanket up close to my chin and with a panic I asked him, "What is wrong?" He rushed to my side lifting me out the bed, leaning me against the wall and told me, "Crystal, listen to me-I love you; I can't lose you." I had a look of confusion and asked him to tell me what was going on. He told me there is only one Naco in the streets of Toledo and that was his father's brother, Bernardino.

I sat down becoming aware of this whole mess. I remember wondering, how the fuck did this just happen to me? Out of everyone in this world, I fall in love with a man who could possibly be my first cousin. I started crying and Lyfe grabbed a hold of my face gently and told me we were never telling anyone what we put together.

CHAPTER 34

"MIRROR" Lil Wayne

Time went by and his family started questioning my background, finding out quickly I had no clue who my father was and that my mom was a drifter. I resembled everyone, and that's what caused them to ask questions. Soon it came out between both sides of our families, and we were left with unforbidden love.

His sisters and mother pushed the subject and sent a picture of me to their uncle who was doing time in prison for murder. The man claimed he remembered my mother and that I looked just like this stranger. So, I flew out to the West Coast and met with this man and more of this family. I was born with jet black hair that turned frizzy and kinky, dimples on both sides of my cheeks and long dark eye lashes. I grew to become a beautiful young lady, with olive skin. I stood 5'3. So, I knew who ever this mystery man was, he would look just like I described myself.

I walked into this huge prison truanting into another lion's den with no fear, only curiosity. When I sat down in front of this man, I instantly started studying his face. I saw his hair was the same texture, and we both shared the exact dimples. Everything was lining up with my own face. I was staring at a stranger's face that looked just like mine. I couldn't fucking believe it. After all this time, I found the missing link in my story, in the most twisted way possible.

I was visiting and meeting everyone. I was blessed to meet his mother Amanda - what a beautiful woman she was. She kept an apron wrapped around her waist and a kitchen that was always cooking something, and smelled like heaven. I stood by her side 90% of the time I spent with her. I loved her instantly and she loved me as well.

When I first arrived at her home, she was standing outside with her daughter waiting for me to pull up and when I did, she started crying. Speaking Spanish, hugging me and pushing my hair behind my ears, she was a beautiful short stern older woman. She did not back down from anything in life and had a soul full of faith. I was very blessed to have met her.

I flew back home. Lyfe and myself were staying away from each another, trying to figure all this out. I started feeling dizzy, like I felt when I got pregnant with Corie, so I ran to the store to grab a test. I took it right away and that's when I found out I was pregnant with my son. I was afraid if I admitted I was pregnant with Lyfe's son, everyone would talk me out of having him. Nothing was stopping me from having this child. I told Lyfe he wasn't the father, but he knew he was. This storm took my breath away.

CHAPTER 35

"YOU BROKE ME FIRST" Tate McRae

Lyfe got sentenced and I was left alone taking care of everything alone. Being in prison made it easy for Lyfe and myself to stay away from one another. No matter how I felt, we knew we couldn't be together. Everything happens for a reason; I am a huge believer in this. Being with him was not a walk in the park. He loved his money, and he loved his women. The universe always reminded me that no matter how lost I got being with that man, I was very aware we weren't going to last. Even before we found out about the possibilities in both our lives, I just ignored reality for the rush he gave me.

My son was one of my greatest blessings and I'm happy I never listened to anyone when they ended up trying to talk me into an abortion. Lyfe became a great father to our son and stepped up for Corie as well. We co-parented for many years.I still looked up to him throughout the years believing in my heart that he respected me. In the end I found out the hard way that man had absolutely no respect for me. Between being hauled into the detective offices with them trying to get me to admit he was still selling drugs, and trying to get him on human trafficking, and then being hauled back in because Clark was involved in a shooting and the detectives were told I was there during these incidents.

I told the officers that were begging me to snitch these two men out. I looked right in their faces and told them to kiss my ass and call my lawyer.

They went on telling me how the father of my children's loyalty wasn't as loyal as mine. I never listened to anyone's advice when it came to what those two men taught me: that was to always keep your mouth shut.

CHAPTER 36

"SPEND A LITTLE DOE" Lil Kim

My loyalty for them got me put into boot camp with a felony on my record. Child custody papers from both after raising my children on my own. Corie was 17 years old and Adrian was 13. I was thrown into jail with disbelief in what I read in my indictment packet. I sat in the county jail reading how these two men wrote out statements to send me to prison for at least a year.

Corie was tired of our reckless lives and her mother's horrible decisions. My son never seen his mother and father fighting and all of a sudden, he was in a middle of a custody battle. None of us had been apart before, and now he was faced with being separated from his mother and sister.

When they surrounded my house, I was finally walked away from both Clark and Lyfe for good. I cleaned the house, sat back, and lit up a blunt to smoke when I heard and felt every cop in Lima Ohio, and what sounded like kicking down my doors, yelling, "I know you're in there Crystal, let us in or we're coming in".

Once again, I couldn't believe what was happening. I hit the blunt a couple of times and stood up to open my back door, giving me more time to smoke and think.

When I opened the door, I was told I was under arrest under a secret indictment. I kept asking them what the charges were. The officer handed me my paperwork. I was never told what they got me for, until I read what my paperwork said. I was being charged with grand theft by deception. I was looking at 5 years, but I was told the laws changed about felony 4 and 5. I received 10 months and signed Adrian to his father and Corie to hers.

I did my time and walked out of that jail alone. It was a breath of fresh air, and I knew I had a lot of work ahead of me. The day before I went in, I ran into Lyfe and Adrian, and I asked him why he was doing this to me. I begged him to tell me and all he could do was bawl his eyes out. That was the last time I ever spoke to him. It's been 10 years since I spoke to either of my children's fathers.

CHAPTER 37

"HOW COULD YOU LEAVE US" Nf

I took a few years pondering on what I put up with and what I brushed under the rug when it came to Clark and Lyfe. That pondering led me to the dark side.

When I got out, I went and searched for the drug money I had put away, to find my secret spot empty. I was furious. I could not believe my eyes. My heart started racing and I felt my anger growing. One person knew where I hid my money, and that was my mother.

I drove over to her house and started yelling up at her window, "Mom I know you're up there! Answer the door!" That day was the hottest day of the year, August. It was hot with no breeze, but at that moment I felt a breeze that brought chills up my spine. I turned my mother's doorknob. To my surprise it was unlocked. I started walking up the stairs and once I reached the top that led into her living room, I stood there with utter shock and disbelief. Mom was sitting on her couch; her head was laying on the coffee table and both arms were hanging towards the floor with a needle stuck in her right arm. I ran to her and realized once my hands touched her - she was gone.

My mother used my drug money to buy the heroin that took her life. I was paralyzed by that memory for years. I blamed myself for the reason we lost our mother. My heart was in pieces from the pain. I was told by Craig and Cassie that mom started using heroin while I was locked up. All I could think about was, if I had listened to her when she used to tell me to stop trusting Clark and Lyfe, maybe I could have saved her by chasing everyone off.

I went back to school that year and all I did was study, read and research everything I could get my hands on. I was an uneducated woman with no diploma, and I had to start somewhere. I went to our local G.E.D center and signed up to take the test.

When I passed it, I was offered the position of Ohio's First Woman Ambassador for Adult Education. I flew out to Arizona and spoke to 5,000 plus people telling them my story. Smiling in a crowd of people wasn't the hard part, believing I deserved it was the issue.

CHAPTER 38

"I'M SICK OF TRYING" Vaboh

During all my troubles I was able to help many people in their own need for peace. I managed to help thousands find their path to get to peace. I went to college to become a social worker for mental health and drug addiction, and during that time I ran into an old friend named Lee.

This guy I used to call one of my greatest friends. I saw him and it brought joy. The last time I heard about Lee he got into trouble with the law for selling drugs and went to prison. So, seeing he made it out, made me smile and when he took one good look at me, I saw he also was happy to see me.

He asked me what I was doing later that evening, I told him I was watching the game. With shock across his face, he said "Well so am I." I invited him over to watch the game with me, a mistake in the making. Lee and I jumped into not just a relationship but less than 30 days later, we were married.

I remember standing outside, calling an old friend. I told her I did not want to do it. She laughed it off thinking I was being my usual jokester. But I wasn't. I was very serious. I went through with it.

Once again, I kept a smile on my face, and no one ever knew I was screaming inside. Things started going wrong the night of the marriage. Lee took my brand-new car and wrecked it. I knew that was another sign I had no business being married to this man. To be honest I wanted the love I was missing from everyone before Lee.

I was literally reaching out to anyone who gave me a glimpse of that feeling. Less than 30 days after I said I do, Lee started beating me up. I was so embarrassed. I did not want to tell anyone, keeping it hidden was the tricky part. I walked around with two black eyes that were always swollen. The first time Lee beat me up, I found out he was reaching out to an old girlfriend.

When I went to comfort him, he pretended to walk away from me while I was yelling, He turned back at me so quickly punching me in the face. My whole body spun around, and I landed headfirst in the couch. Every time I tried to get back up, Lee would start punching on me to keep me down. I have never been hit the way that man hit me. I still remember the cries that came out with every punch to my head and face.

CHAPTER 39

"GANGSTA" Kehlani

I would have left him, but I was too embarrassed to reach out to anyone. My family I had left, was upset when I got married without telling anyone. Everyone thought I lost my mind when I did it. They were probably right.

By the 3rd time Lee beat me up, it was so bad, I had to call 911. I was sleeping in our bed and Lee was out getting drunk. He walked in, saw dinner was not made and he was pissed. He walked into our bedroom and grabbed me by my hair dragging me out of our bed and throughout the house. He started punching and kicking me badly! I was trying to hang on to the walls in hopes he would stop dragging me.

That was a mistake because once I did that, he started ripping my clothes off me. I looked at him with pure fear in my eyes begging him to see it was me. He shook his head long enough to release me from his grip. I quickly grabbed my phone and ran outside screaming for help with nothing to cover my body. I jumped in my car and called 911. The police came right away and dragged him out the house and into the cop car.

This was 3 months into our fresh marriage and I was worse off than ever. I had to drop out of college due to the black eyes. I lost both my vehicles with Lee wrecking them and using them for drug runs. I bought a nice trailer. When I married Lee, the park managers did not like that he was a black man, so she managed to rob me for the trailer I bought with my own cash. I had no fight in me.

One day I started crying. Gelly was sitting next to me while I started screaming, "Leave me alone!" She asked me who I was talking to, and I told her God. I said, "I just want him to leave me alone! I just want to be normal." She offered me a place to live, and when Lee got out a week later, I took him back. With every sweet nothing that came out his mouth, with every "I'm sorry," I decided to give him another chance.

Three days later I was fighting for my life. Every word he pleaded to me to believe, was a lie. Lee had me give him the money to buy him the drugs he needed to sell. Then he taught me how to weigh everything up and bag it up for the people he had coming to my house. I guess one of those people started calling him, bitching about the sacks I gave to her. This girl told him it was not a big enough sack for what she paid for, so when he got off the phone, he told me to stop folding clothes and look at him.

CHAPTER 40

"NEEDED ME" Rihanna

I instantly saw how mad he was. I begged him not to get upset. I already knew the consequences of his anger. Pointing that out to Lee was also a mistake because he flew over the bed and grabbed me by my neck! Lifting me up with both his hands, strangling me while whispering in my ear that he was killing me tonight!

I knead him between his legs and it gave me enough time to take a deep breath! He swung my body around, landing me on the bed so he could climb on top of me! I could not breathe; I was even losing my hearing. I saw the devil in his eyes, and I knew he was going to kill me! I reached for his eyes, and he clinched down on my fingers biting them until my blood was dripping out his mouth! I was unconscious when Gelly ran upstairs to see if everything was ok. She told me she found Lee on top of me strangling me and she used all her might to get him off me!

She also stated her dad had to help her drag him off me and Lee was fighting them to come finish me off. I was rushed to the same hospital I was visiting throughout these few months of being married to this guy. The nurses knew me. They knew I was getting beat up. No matter what type of excuse I made up in hopes that they didn't know.

When I was rushed into the E.R, they shut the E.R down forbidding any males to enter the building. The police were called, and Lee got away. I woke up in the hospital screaming in fear. I was dreaming he found me. There was a nurse sitting next to me trying to calm me down, telling me that I was in a safe place. She was in tears, and asked me once I got discharged from the hospital, to promise her that I would divorce him and never come back. She stated, if I came back, it would be in a body bag.

The L.P.D came to the hospital to take me to the courthouse to sign paperwork to send Lee to prison. The same dirty detective that always harassed me due to Corie's father Clark, was sitting in the room. He told me I could trust him this time and he would send him to prison for 2 to 8 years. I signed the paperwork after they told me they found Lee sneaking behind Gelly's house. They said he was trying to break into her house to finish me off.

CHAPTER 41

"Saddest Day" Foxy Brown

The day before court, detective Steve Stec called my phone and told me I did not need to show up to court because they were not charging Lee. I started crying, asking him why he wasn't being charged. He told me it was because apparently Lee brought up an ex-boyfriend who was in some trouble. The detective said unless I told him what he needed to know, he was not going to help me.

I hung up the phone, and laid in tears. I had no one in my corner or nowhere to run. I was in complete fear of my life. Lee received 10 days served in the D.V case and had to stay for 80 days for missing child support court. I was devastated. I could not even count on the police.

I was given a number 419-228-HELP from a domestic violence advocate. After looking at the walls for what seemed like months, I picked up the phone and called them bawling my eyes out. I asked them to please help me. The Cross Road Crisis Center saved my sanity. The state of shock had finally hit me, and fear grew even stronger. I was holding on for dear life, in every way possible. The first night I went to the shelter I tried sleeping but it was hard. I walked to the living room and fell asleep on their couch. Clients weren't allowed to sleep out in the living room, so I'm blessed they allowed me to. They were wonderful women, and never left my side. I was safe for the first time since being with my grandparents. I started going to groups they offered, and I started participating. After a couple of months, I started thinking about how I messed up college, so I did everything I could to try and get accepted back.

I was told that I needed to write an essay to the college officials explaining why I had dropped out. So, I did. I poured my heart out with every truth in me and the passion I held within me to go back to school and learn something new.

CHAPTER 42

"GODS & MONSTERS" Lana Del Rey

What they had no clue about was that I was holding onto the only positive I had left inside of me. Growing up, I did not have time to read books, nor did I have a lot of people jumping to my aid, let alone reading to me.

College was the source that made me realize how much I missed out on at school, and how much I loved every bit of learning. Like my children, books kept me grounded from stepping into any shit. I had lost all hope in mankind, so when I read a book, I felt safe and in a happy place. I was a torn down young lady, who kept a smile on her face. However, when I was home alone, I started self-medicating with crack cocaine. I honestly did not see the harm of being home and smoking a couple balls. I didn't have the kids with me.

I lost everyone who would have cared. I was more lost than I ever before. I felt like as long as I accomplished a lot, and held on, I was not hurting anyone. I had no clue I was hurting myself. I hid it from everyone as much as I could, but the longer I kept using drugs, the more people found out. I started caring less who found out. I was offered to become certified in the state of Ohio to become a Peer Supporter for mental health and drug addiction. I took all the classes I needed to take and passed all my test with flying colors. I loved everything about those two subjects, how couldn't I love it? I was living the lifestyle for 30 plus years.

I lost a lot of great people, family and friends due to mental health and drug addictions. I needed to find myself. I needed to know what the fuck was wrong with me and why I could not get a break in life. During another upcoming achievement, I was excepted back at school. I had all intentions to finish what I started, but here I was taking on more.

I divorced Lee, and I found a cute apartment that I was able to rent from an old man who loved starring at my breasts. With eviction I received from my ex in laws, all I could do is smile in hopes my tits would get me this apartment. Which they did. But gosh dealing with another weirdo trying to pay me for sex was tiring. So, I tried keeping to myself, and focused on college and the Peer Program.

 I went out with Elizabeth one night and I ran into a guy I crushed on when I was a kid. He came right up to me and told me I looked exactly the same as I did when we were kids. I smiled and thanked him. His name was Joseph, and man I loved looking at this man.

CHAPTER 43

"SERIAL KILLER" Lana Del Rey

It brought back memories when I was a kid. He used to ride his bike in front of me for hour's, showing off. I was too shy to ever say anything, so I would sit on my porch and watch him. Joseph grazed my hand and said, "I'm no boy anymore, I'm a grown ass man. I see you turned out to be a beautiful women Crystal."

He had me and I did not resist it. I gave him my number and went home that night. By the time I made it safely to my bed, he was already calling me. I noticed I was starting to be clingy to anyone who came into my life. I still had no clue what I was doing in life, besides holding onto the part of my soul that wasn't dark.

I was a single soul with wings ready to fly away at any moment. Every time I thought to myself, I had nothing left to live for, I pictured my children living without me, like I was living without my mother.

Those thoughts kept me somewhat stricter on how far I would take my party life. I went out as much as possible. I would walk into class hung over and in pain from everything I consumed the night before. Rich men flocked to me and remembering what Lyfe taught me, I used what I had to get every penny I could out of those motherfuckers. To me they were scum. Men made me sick and the things they asked me to do made me sicker.

So, I didn't just listen to what Lyfe taught me, but what I witnessed from every woman in my life. The women in my life were wolves in sheep's clothing. Every one of them were my aunts and I had 8 of those beauties. On one side they were long hair blonde bombshells with blue and green eyes and a strong hand like no other. Rolling around in drop top Corvettes and Mercedes Benz. They walked around with fur coats with class and mouths like sailors. Every man that walked their paths got chewed up and spit out.

The other side, they had bodies like a goddess, curvy but slim and legs that didn't end. Tan skin and amber eyes, long black hair that reached down to their butts. Gangster as they come, and equally classy, robbing men while looking right in their eyes hypnotizing them with their beauty. These were the women I learned from that I didn't have to do anything I didn't want to. We were a rare breed of women and we got what we wanted. Torturing these types of men filled a void and became very addictive. I started seeing not just how easy it was to bat my pretty amber eyes to get whatever I wanted, but how this too was warring on my soul. Stopping wasn't an option though.

CHAPTER 44

"BE CAREFUL" Cardi B

Joseph took me on a few dates and when I finally invited him over, he never left. We got married shortly after, and this time it was 3 months into this disaster. I came to find out this man just got out of prison for beating his ex-wife so badly she had to get reconstructive surgery to her face. Again, red flags I was ignoring.

The day we got married I made sure I drank a bottle of liquor. The ceremony was short once again and no one knew about it, not even his family. He worked 3rd shift while I worked first shift plus college fulltime. I had 40 hours to finish to get certified for the Peer Support Program. Three days after we were married, I received a phone call from a female telling me she's been sleeping with my now husband. She said she felt she needed to let me know what he was doing behind my back. I asked her how this could be when we were always together? She went on and explained how when I was in college or at work Joseph would drive my red truck over to her house.

I also was told he was telling not just this random woman we were not married, but also his family. He told his family I was nuts and forged the marriage certificate. Every one of them believed it. I fucking couldn't believe this mother fucker was lying to everyone and living two different lives. I was devastated. I was beyond words, and I felt myself ticking like a time bomb. After that first phone call explaining I was sleeping with a complete stranger, 17 more females contacted me with the same disloyal stories and disbelief. Some of these females were nice to me and many threatened my life, and others felt like it was a competition.

I had 40 hours I had to get done. I remember driving to an empty building, parking my car, collecting my thoughts. Talking myself out of going home and shooting this mother fucker. He was another man I opened up to about my life and I knew right there, I no longer trusted myself. I made it through those 40 hours, and I started my career as a mental health and drug addiction advocate. I had a 21-case load and every clinic I had, loved me. I also cared dearly for them; they took my mind off all my troubles. I was doing something productive and I loved every bit of it. The closer I got to them the more emotional I got. I started realizing I could not help anyone if I was living my life the way I was.

The guilt started building up. I could not be the reason why someone couldn't deal with life, if I gave them the wrong advice. I was still wrapping my head around another upcoming divorce. Joseph was calling up to my place of business telling them I was getting high. I decided that I needed to step back before I got myself branded for life. I went home that night and kicked Joseph out. He roughed me up a little, putting fear in my soul, but he did leave. I thought to myself, I could handle any type of abuse after everything I've survived.

CHAPTER 45

"MY MEDICINE" The Pretty Reckless

After having Emma, I started counseling and was put on medication. I started seeing a phycologist, which was one of the first officials who pushed himself on me. He told me I wouldn't need medication forever and that he would buy me and the kids a home, a computer, and a nice car if I would show him my bare body.

I later found out he was overdosing me with medication. I was asked by Lutheran Social Services higher above if something was going on and if I needed to talk about it. I thought really hard about how no one ever believed me after they promised I wouldn't be blamed. Once again, I took a chance and told a room full of employers what Dr. Trevino was doing to me and what he promised me if I did it. I'll tell you what happened. They added windows in every doctor's office since that was where it all happened and ended up changing the name to Colemans. I however was left with more trauma, and more trust issues.

Wondering if I should have kept my mouth closed, I might have been able to take the abuse long enough to secure my children and myself. When I was 16 years old, I was placed in J.D.C for keeping Clark's secret on a shooting. I was told if I kept the secret when Clark received a settlement that was awarded to him, his mother would pay for Corie's college and set her up, making sure she got what she needed.

I was also told by the detectives if I did not tell on Clark, I would never see my daughter take her first steps. My loyalty ran deep but most of all I couldn't leave my baby without. I got caught and sat in the juvenal detention center. My name was called by a doctor for an exam. That doctor stuck two fingers inside me bare handed, one in my vagina the other in my butt, looked at me and said," Good girl, you're not a little slut, are you? "

I wanted to kick him in the face, but I was already attacked by 5 male guards. So, I kept my mouth shut. He went on telling me I had breasts that could feed a village.

Trusting doctors has not been the easiest on my end. Just like the lies that came out a man's mouth - they were the same lies that was brushed under the rug in the whole city of Lima, Ohio. If the police didn't like you, you paid for it by them never helping you. They looked at you like you were dirt. You were judged by who your parents were and what trouble you were ever involved in. That's why I worked so hard to make a difference through my career until I could not take my own devils winning in my own life.

CHAPTER 46

"AUNT DOT" Lil Kim

I stepped away from everything and everyone that ever hurt me, and walked into a lifestyle that would take your life. I was at the point where I said "Fuck life and everyone I ever had encounters with." I no longer had the strength to beg for my children's forgiveness. I had no more self-worth after being abused all my life and watching it get brushed under the rug. My fear disappeared and I no longer wanted to feel my heartbeat. I packed up my life and put everything I owned into storage. I hit a home boy up and told him I needed to make some money and I was coming that way.

When I pulled into town, I went to a bar a girlfriend was bartending at. I ordered a beer and looked at the first man I knew had a pocket full of money. I saw him looking me up and down while walking up to me. He asked if I would like to sit with him. I said, "And why would I do that with the likes of you?" He giggled and told me he could make all my dreams come true. I looked at my girl and nodded my head, which meant I got one on the hook, keep the liquor flowing.

The more he spoke, the drunker I got and pushed shots down his throat. When a man yearns for a wild soul like me that meant they needed some fire. In hopes that I would lay my sins all over their bodies. Whatever smirk I gave him and whisper I spoke in his ear, made him crave my dark side. He handed me 20,000. I spent two days with him, keeping him up with cocaine and liquor. I linked up with my home boy, grabbed an ounce of crack cocaine and went to my niece's.

That was the only place I felt safe, and I knew no one would find me. She told me I could sleep in her spare room. So, I set up shop, started selling dope and smoking it. Sleep ended for me. I was looking for a way to dissolve my human life. I put pieces on my crack pipe that was as big as my thumb, in hopes of having a heart attack with each hit. Days turned to weeks, and weeks turned to months. I was still alive, with little food in my stomach, sitting in a room I never came out of.

My daughter called me one day and asked me what I was doing, I told her I've been in Lima for a while and I was not sure what my plans were. Corie started crying and told me to stop lying to her. She said, "Mom I know what you're doing, I'm not stupid!" That day I explained to her I never lied to her. I was trying to protect her from any more bullshit her mother caused in her life. I asked her not to worry about me, and whatever happened I would be fine.

CHAPTER 47

"THE PURGE" Demetrius X"

Corie told me she could not help but to worry and she wanted me to forgive myself and others. I did not have the guts to tell her that I had no emotion left to forgive anyone, let alone myself.

A couple of hours went by, and the phone rang. I rushed to answer it. I heard a familiar voice on the other end, "Jen is this you?" She said, "In the flesh," then asked me, what I've been doing. I told her I was losing my mind. She told me to get dressed. She said, "I'm on my way to get you."

When she showed up, she already had a sack in one pocket and a bottle of liquor next to her. She asked me what was wrong. I looked at her and said, "Shit what isn't wrong?" She asked me if I wanted to take a ride out to a friend's house to party. I told her "Yeah why not." We headed out to Shawnee and drove to this beautiful home.

When we walked to the door, there he stood, I could not believe it, it was my dentist. He was very welcoming and showed us where we could sit. I remember Jen and him walking towards the back of the house. Jen came rushing out and told me she would be right back, and I could stay there. Ken told me I was welcome to stay, and he wouldn't bite. He had no clue I was the biter.

He poured me some wine and took me down in his basement to play ping pong. He told me Jen went to grab him an 8 balls of crack cocaine. When she returned, we all stayed at his house getting high. I had to leave the next morning, so Ken walked me out and asked if I would have dinner with him sometime. I told him I wasn't sure about that. He handed me a piece of paper with his number on it and I drove off. On the way home I thought about what had happened. I was literally partying with my dentist who now was asking me out to dinner. Life was starting to make sense in the darkest way. I thought, "So if a person has authority, they use it to their advantage?" Everyone I went to for help, took advantage of the fact that I was uneducated and poor. And every lesson Lyfe gave me about selling my soul for money, suddenly made sense to me. This world I stepped into was either *eat or be eaten*. I was full of revenge and ready to purge.

CHAPTER 48

"WHORE" In This Moment

I was standing in my shower letting the hot water hit my body, leaning against the wall. My soul had drifted so far away that I wasn't sure if I even had one at that point. Every man I trusted took advantage of me, and stole the one thing I had left, *my children*.

When I saw that my daughter had no respect left for me, I told myself I had no reason to live. When I watched the females, I once called my sisters, rob me blind with no regard to anything I was going through, I turned cold. When I handed my daughter over for adoption to strangers and not one person on either side of our families would help me, I lost my mind. When I walked in my mother's home to fight her for stealing my drug money and found her dead from an overdose, I turned numb.

Every time I went to a doctor's office of some kind, and was sexually abused, I turned more hateful towards men. I saw how ugly the world was and how I was getting the blunt of it all. I was sick and tired of taking everyone's shit. I was done raising children and raising grown men who never loved me. I started feeling like a pit stop for every asshole on this planet. The rumors I heard about myself were so ugly and hateful, I had nothing more to say. I quit trying to stick up for myself when I realized it was my own blood, my best friends, the men I bared children with, and the motherfuckers I married. I stood in that shower thinking of everything that has ever hit me in the gut and I told myself it was time, time for revenge.

I got out the shower and got dressed. Ironically, I had a dentist appointment. When I showed up, I noticed the ladies working there whispering and starring in my direction. I thought this mother fucker had to have told them something. I was called in the back and once I stepped through those doors, Ken was standing there, waiting with a huge smile.

He did not shy away from letting everyone know he wanted me. Ken took me to his office and sat me down. He explained his life in a nutshell and offered me a position to take in it. He had five other girlfriends and he paid for them all. He told me he would give me an allowance every week, which meant picking up a check from his office as an employee written out to me. I had no job, and nothing left to live for, so I accepted his offer. He handed me a check written out for one thousand five hundred dollars. He told me to go cash it at his bank in Wapakoneta. He handed me an American Express card and told me to buy new cloths because he could not be seen with me wearing ripped jeans.

Before I walked out his office, he handed me a set of keys to his Range Rover and told me to be at his home at 7 pm sharp. I did everything he told me to do. I can't lie, it gave me a rush of power I never felt before.

CHAPTER 49

"PUFF THE MAGIC DRAGON" Peter & Mary

I never had to go out and buy drugs. Ken made sure whoever sold them to us, would also deliver them to his house. He always tipped the drug dealer as if he was the butler. There was so much money coming through my fingers, I did not have time to spend it.

I started sending my daughter thousands of dollars to take care of herself and my granddaughter. Every time Corie asked me how I was getting this money I told her not to ask, just take it. I was living a lie and I did not care. The more time I spent with Ken the fatter my pockets got. I quit sleeping, I quit eating. All I did was shop and travel to wherever he would send me. He had five other women and an ex-wife he was taking care of, so when it was their turn to spend time with him, he would always send me to a 5-star suite for a week.

Ken was a very material man; he had the best and made sure I always did as well. My appointments were to the spa, and shopping sprees. We had one drug dealer we dealt with: his name was Jason. Jason was good looking and smelled like heaven. Ken would send Jason along with me making sure I stayed high and happy. Jason was reimbursed every time. Jason came from the same neighborhood as I did, so we knew one another well.

When he found out I was sleeping with Ken, and we smoked crack together, it got his dick hard. To Jason this was a perfect way to make easy money, and sneak behind Kens back with me - every drug dealer's fancy.

I was the ticket to Kens bank account. Jason sat me down and showed me a video he had of Ken smoking crack and told me if I presented this to him, we could get anything we desired. At first, I was all for it, but the longer I was using drugs, I started seeing how much worse my life could get, if I continued. I fought with myself a lot.

Every time I had a chance to hurt the people who hurt me or were hurting me, I couldn't feed into their ways. I was already destroying myself, and the people I was around were more lost than I was. I did not have the heart to destroy anyone else. I stayed up many nights for over a year with Ken, listening to how hurt he was.

This man was twelve years older than me, divorced and lost his family due to mental health and addiction. I was very educated on this subject, but I was so far gone I could not even help him. So, I watched this man cry over losing his children and wife and how he spent time with what he called 'trailer park trash,' to ease the pain. I remember him looking at me and telling me we weren't like 'those people'. He said that a lot.

At first, I did not understand, but after a while I realized he put me on a higher pedestal then the other girls. He started breaking up with the other girls and he moved me in. We spoke about the video of him smoking crack. I was honest. I told him I would do anything to help him so he would not get in any trouble. One of his number 1 rules was that no one was ever allowed to live with him. I was cool with that because I did not want to live with another man ever again.

He started getting heat from the video and I was there to save him from losing his dentistry license and his own private business. He told me to call the dental board and tell the investing officer that Ken did not smoke crack and that I was the one who had the cocaine in his house. We practiced this speech for hours, and I made the call.

When I got off the phone, Ken handed me a credit card and told me to go buy a new car. I looked at him and told him he did not need to buy me a car. I said, "Ken I did that for you because you have more to lose than I do." It did not matter what I said, he kept on repeating himself, and told me again to go buy a car. So, I did.

When I came back home Ken was sitting with a tray full of crack and my favorite bottle of wine, *Kendall Jackson*. We started smoking, and he stood up to use the restroom. I heard a boom, and I ran back to the master bedroom, finding Ken on the ground.

CHAPTER 50

"TOO GOOD AT GOODBYES" Sam Smith

I ran to him using all my might to pick him up and get him to the bed. I told him I was calling 911 and he told me not to. Standing there with the phone in my hand I thought to myself, I better listen. I asked him what happened. He told me it was nothing - he was just dizzy. I ran around, throwing away the drugs and getting him comfortable. I started crying, asking him if he was ok. He looked at me and asked me why I had tears in my eyes. I told him I didn't want anything happening to him. He said with a smart remark, "Awe she does have a heart." That brought a smile to my face. I giggled a little and watched him fall asleep.

The next morning, I found him in his closet crying with faeces all around him and on him. I rushed to his aid and started begging him to let me take him to the hospital. He yelled at me saying, "The party isn't over!" I carried him to the shower. He was so bad that he could not stand up on his own. I got in the shower with him, holding him up and washing his body, while listening to him cry about how he fucked his life up. He kept repeating how thankful he was and how embarrassed he was because I had to do this. I told him not to thank me, and that everything would be ok. I dressed him and put him in the bed.

When I was finished, he told me to call Jason to bring us some crack over. I grabbed his phone and went in the other room. I did not call Jason. I called his mother and told her who I was and when she got a chance, she needed to come to Ken's home and check on him. I went in the master bedroom and asked how he was feeling. He told me he felt like death and asked how long it would be until

Jason got there. I lied to him and told him he would be here later because he was busy. Even though I lived with Ken I made sure I got my own place to live. I knew by now nothing lasted long and by the looks of things, it was coming to an end.

I packed my things into my car while Ken was resting. I made sure he was drinking water and tried feeding him as much as he could get down. I knew something bad was wrong, but I did not know what it was. I never told Ken goodbye or that I was leaving. I waited until his mother showed up before I walked out of Kens life forever.

CHAPTER 51

"RIDE" Lana Del Rey

Ken contacted me when he got out the hospital and told me the doctors told him I saved his life. He thanked me and asked me why I left without speaking to him. I told him it was because I did not want to see someone else die, and I wasn't sure if I wanted to keep living that way. He expressed how he wished he met me years before life bit him. He told me to never forget how important of a woman I was. I told him I wouldn't forget and to take care of himself.

A few months went by and I got a knock on my door from this guy who needed help. Someone was chasing him, so I let him in. When I did, he sat down he asked me if I was still with Ken. I looked at him with confusion and asked him how he knew anything about Ken and I. He went on and told me Ken had him on his payroll and wanted him to check on me. At the time I didn't think anything of it. To me I thought that it was Ken's way of making sure I was ok.

Later I was told Ken had this guy come over for revenge. He was mad that I left and God forbid anyone walk out of his life. I was more naïve than I ever thought. I had no clue people were so evil. The guy Ken sent to my house acted concerned and worried about my wellbeing. He was my age and easy to talk to. I thought he might have been another victim of life, so I welcomed him in.

I did ice for the first time with him. He had it in his pocket and asked me if I wanted to try some. I told him no at first, but he kept sticking it in my face. He literally put the pipe to my lips and told me to slowly hit it, so I did. I leaned back blowing out a dragon cloud of smoke out my lungs, and for the first time in my life, I felt like I was flying. I did not care that I went from smoking crack to smoking meth in a matter of one hit.

I never touched cocaine again. I found the drug that took every bad thing that has ever happened to me away. The men were as much as a drug as the drug itself, along with the money. I learned quickly that all money wasn't good money, so leaving Ken was easy, at least I thought it was.

CHAPTER 52

"ADRENALIZE" In This Moment

That first hit was my newfound love, and I could not get enough of it. I woke up after five days without sleep and felt my body craving crystal meth. Looking at the man who introduced me to this poison, sack dangling in his hand, with pure lust. I knew I fucked up, but it didn't stop me from wanting to feel the adrenalin running through my soul.

I told him to hold the foil and guide my lungs while I inhaled the love I've been longing for. I saw his devilish eyes watching me blow out the cloud of death with ease in his face. Another five days feeling my mind drift away and seeing what I always knew to be true. The shadows started speaking to me. I tried not to talk back, but that only made them mad.

The longer I inhaled the devil's smoke, the more I could not hold back. Letting my family and friends know what I was doing, was a way to warn them I would kill anyone who tried to lead them to where I was. I started to fear the shadows, feeling them kiss my cheeks once I did crash to get some sleep. The noises in my head startled me, so I stood up and went to my bookshelf to draw them out. Grabbing ten books at a time, laying them across my bed, begging them to stop talking inside my head. I opened my first book and couldn't put it down. Next thing I knew three days down, not sleeping, nothing to eat, I was withering way.

I was asked by a girl I knew, if I wanted to go to a gathering. I asked where it was, and she told me at this guy Sean Rader's. I haven't heard this name since Jesse passed away. He was one of his best friends, and someone I always looked at from afar. I remember before life got too hard, I would sit at Rob Park and watch him every Saturday playing football. He never knew I did, but I was too shy to ever speak to him. He was ten years older than me, and never looked my way. The night I walked into his home; our eyes instantly linked.

He was yelling at this guy for trespassing in his yard, and all I could do was smile and tell him I see some things never change. Putting his head down, but still looking up at me, he spoke and said, "Hi Crystal, you look really good".

Finally, after all these years I thought he saw me. I felt this type of joy I could not explain. It wasn't the negative rush I was getting from everything toxic that surrounded me, but a feeling of peace. I looked him dead in his eyes and thanked him with a smile. Looking around I was pleased to see how well Sean was doing. I told him I was proud of him and his home was beautiful. He walked me to each room showing me his hard work. He took a house that was a dump and turned it into a beautiful home. Not once was he touchy feely towards me. He did however look at me a few times and told me how gorgeous I turned out to be.

CHAPTER 53

"IS THAT ALRIGHT" Lady Gaga

Sean saw what I was doing in life and never judged me. He had his own demons he was dealing with. That night at his house party, he saw Frank put the pipe of meth to my lips. He ran up yelling for him to get away from me. I looked at Sean while I inhaled the cloud of death, and I saw the sadness vailing his face. When I started to leave, I noticed Sean following me to my car and I asked him, "What's wrong?" He told me nothing was wrong, he just wanted to make sure I made it to my car safely. I can't lie, I instantly thought it was strange. He never touched me, he never got weird with me, so I was instantly suspicious towards him.

I kept Frank around for about 3 weeks and as usual things got weird quick. Frank started getting strange and angry with me. He would snatch the keys out my hands and drag me back into my house when I would try and leave. I didn't know who to call or even reach out to, so I dialed Sean's number and to my surprise he answered. He sounded so happy, but his happiness changed quickly when he heard me on the other end crying. His voice got strict and he calmly asked me what was wrong. I started crying harder and apologized for calling him. He asked me where Frank was. I explained he was in the house. Sean knew right then I could not say too much. He told me he was leaving work and coming over.

I hung up the phone and within 1.5 seconds Sean was banging at my door. Frank rushed to the door and greeted him, with a, "What's up bro?" Sean pushed him out the way asking him where I was. I spoke up and said, "I'm right here Sean!" I had my purse wrapped around both shoulders with tears falling down my cheeks. He grabbed both my arms gently asked me if I was ok. I shook my head no. He looked at Frank and asked him if there was some where he needed to go.

When Frank realized Sean was there for me, he started screaming, "She's crazy." Sean told him to grab his shit so that he could drop him off somewhere other than at my house. Frank told him he wasn't going anywhere. Sean turned to look at me and asked me nicely to walk into my room and turn my music on. Something in his approach made me trust what he asked me to do. I went into my room and turned on my radio. Sitting there, I was worried that I made a bad choice by calling him over. I started over-thinking everything, thinking of the worst-case scenarios. Sean was selling drugs at the time and we were all using then. We came from a town where the county officials hated us, and instead of trying to help us, they went against us like they received commission.

It was too late to change what I did so, I thought whatever happens, happens. Next thing I knew, I heard a tap on my bedroom door and Sean spoke up making me aware he was coming in. He stood by my door, never fully entering my bedroom, telling me it was safe to come out. I looked at him with confusion and relief. Sean always seemed to be able to read me well. He put my mind at ease and told me Frank's ride was on its way. I did not know what to say. I was happy but embarrassed. I took care of myself - I never had anyone sticking up for me, let alone showing up to my aid.

CHAPTER 54

"I NEED YOU" Lynyrd Skynyrd

Sean seen the fear I held in my eyes from life's curveballs thrown at me. This man never left my side and became the greatest friend of my life. He tippy toed around me for over a year, knowing with one wrong move, I would run away; which I did many times. Trusting people in general was hard, but trusting a man was even worse. He knew this. I knew one day Sean would walk out my life like everyone before him did, so I kept myself safe by hiding behind a wall.

I always thought it was suspicious Sean never tried sleeping with me, but instead he started showing up fixing things around my house. He knew I never left my residence, so he always made time to stop by and check on me. One day he asked me if he could take me to lunch, I said yes. He was so excited to take me to this chicken spot that had the best chicken in Lima, Ohio, *Cottons*. He knew I wasn't eating for obvious reasons, but anytime he was around he made sure I was.

Sean took me to the park with the chicken he had bought for us and would make me laugh so hard - something I quit doing years ago. I was living in active addiction for over two years, and I didn't have any plans to stop. I remember looking at Sean asking him why he was so nice to me. He looked me in my eyes and said, "Crystal, because you're a lady, and men are supposed to treat ladies nicely". I fell in love with Sean at that moment, but I no longer trusted myself, so I never told him.

I pushed him away, making anything up I could in my head to make sure I kept Sean away. Some might think I did that to protect myself, but I actually was protecting him. The longer I ignored his calls, I found myself getting higher and falling into a deeper depression. One night I got a call from my cousin all upset. Him and I had a lot in common - we didn't trust people and we both walked the shadows of hell. He told me his mom had passed away and when the funeral was. We both kind of sat on the phone in shock and agreed neither of us would go to the funeral.

The morning of the funeral I heard my niece banging on my door yelling, "Let me in Aunt Crystal!" She was the one person in my life I never hid from or ignored. I knew what it was about: my aunts funeral. I let her in, and she told me to get dressed. I was going to the funeral. She looked at me and said, "Aunt Crystal, I need you." When she said those words, I grabbed a black dress and threw it on. I was bitching, telling her she knew how I can't deal with these kinds of things, but it didn't matter what I said, she wasn't leaving without me. She told me Sean was with my cousin and promised to make sure he would take him to the funeral. Once I heard Sean would be there, I knew that I would be ok, so I jumped in my car and drove there.

CHAPTER 55

"SHALLOW" Lady Gaga

My niece Erin Lee expressed her concerns on how much weight I had lost. She told me that I needed to get myself together. I made a joke to take her mind off everything she was facing that day. The last thing I wanted her to do was to be worried about me. When I pulled up, I looked for Sean in the parking lot, but I didn't see him. So, I took a deep breath and started walking towards the door of the funeral home. I felt a panic attack coming over me, so I sat on a bench outside. My head was hanging low, and my hands started shaking. Then I heard a familiar voice say, "Hey brat." Lifting my head, I saw Sean standing there.

 I jumped up and ran into his arms. He wrapped his arms so gently around me that I felt a sense of home. My face smothered in his chest, exhaling my sadness and sorrows, he asked me how I was doing. I told Sean that I missed him, and I apologized for being so mean. His famous words to me were, "You were forgiven the moment you yelled at me." I started crying with relief, happy he was still willing to be my friend. He took my hand and wrapped it under his arm. He walked me into the funeral home to show my respects and say my goodbyes to my aunt D. That night he stayed with me, holding me in his arms. I woke up in a panic, no longer in Sean's arms. I popped up with heavy breathing confused and looking for

Sean. He was sitting on a chair outside my bedroom watching me sleep. He gave me a calming smile, telling me I was safe and to lay back down. He walked over to me, covering me up with my blanky that I had held on to since my mother passed away, and kissed me on my forehead. Rubbing his fingers through my hair, he whispered, "Everything's going to be ok."

I slept for 16 hours and when I woke up Sean was carrying in groceries. I looked lost, wondering why he was doing these things for me. I never said too much, worrying if I did, it would only scare him away. Sean watched me lay in my bed for days and sometimes months. He would worry often, but with disregard of how he felt, I was still patiently waiting for the day I was going to lose my only friend. The more time I spent with him the more I didn't trust myself which always came out as me not trusting him.

One night we were partying, and we got news: one of our mutual friends just got popped. Word on the streets was this friend gave Sean's name to the police. I sat there, ear hustling the conversation Sean was having with this guy and I lost it. I started bawling my eyes out, telling him he had to stop selling drugs because they were coming after him. I started uncontrollably begging him, expressing that if something happened to him, I would be thrown to the wolves. I told him if he had to stop being around me to stay safe then I understood.

I felt like everything I touched was bound to fall apart or be taken from me. The thought of something happening to Sean hit me in the gut and all my feelings came out of nowhere. He ran to my side, grabbed my hand and said, "Crystal, I would stop selling drugs before I ever stayed away from you."

CHAPTER 56

"SAVE ME" Jelly Roll

Sean told everyone they had to leave that night. He walked everyone out my door and walked back to my bedroom, climbed into my bed, and moved me close enough to wrap his arms around me. I was still crying, not having much faith that he would stop selling drugs. He gently wiped my tears away and kissed me for the first time on my lips. Everything in that moment no longer mattered to me. That was the first time him and I made love. He had no clue that was my first time ever making love.

I knew this man had lived a life of pain, and I knew no matter what type of pain he endured he was still a beautiful man with a huge heart. I could not be the reason that Sean Rader would go to prison. I looked at him sleeping, and I whispered, "I love you." As many times as I have ever told someone I loved them, this time was different, I knew it was different. I also knew if I kept using drugs, Sean would never step away from selling them. He was always so worried that someone would hurt me by giving me some bad shit, and so many people we knew were dying left, right and center. There was only one way out, I had to leave him.

Leaving Sean was going to be hard. My heart tore to pieces the moment I knew what needed to be done. The first thing I thought was as soon as I left the man I truly loved; he'll never know how much he met to me. After listening to his story and knowing this man's background, I knew he's never been loved probably. Him and I lived a similar life - I could see it in his eyes. He didn't see the beauty of his heart. I felt like I had to protect him, not just from me, but from the mother fuckers trying to take him down. I watched us withering away from every hit we took and I forced myself to feel hate towards him. Not the hate you feel when someone does you wrong, but the type of hate you feel when the one person in your life doesn't give up on you, and he was my person. I loved this man, and I didn't know how to show him how deeply until I went and got help.

I watched this man stay awake to make sure I slept. I watched this man walk miles in the cold and snow to check on my safety. I saw the love and resilience of his strength when I woke up in the middle of the night screaming from everything that ever took a piece of my soul. I could not fail him like others have, and I had no clue where to start. I started having spiritual awakenings that enabled me to see the future ahead of me, and what I saw was beautiful.

However, if I could not have Sean healthy and safe along with me, I didn't want anything at all. I never chose a man over family and friends; they always came first. Seeing my mother choose men over her children made me sick, so it became a habit by fault. I say that because Sean was the only one who stood his ground with me. He fed me when I wanted to die and he stood by my side in silence when I needed him.

I laugh at the time I called him on the phone, calmly explaining I needed him at my house. At the time I was too embarrassed to tell him I feared the dark and I thought someone was outside sneaking around my house. Sean showed up and as I opened the door, I started crying telling him I knew someone was trying to hurt me. I must be honest I was very high, malnourished and I hadn't slept for five days. Sean saw the fear in my eyes, grabbed a stick that was close by and took me by my hand walking me outside. He started screaming, "Motherfucker you better leave Crystal alone". Then he started hitting all my bushes, telling this imaginary ghost he would beat him to death if he scared me again. I went from scared to death to falling, laughing so hard my belly ached.

This man reminded me so much of my grandpa Max, never giving up on me or making fun of me being scared. A week went by and I knew Sean was going to be busy. I had a plan to put everything in storage and leave without a word. I got everything in storage and my ride showed up. I started changing my mind about leaving. Josh who became my saving grace, threw me over his shoulder, telling me I was coming with him and I was getting help. I kicked and I screamed yelling at him, "I can't leave Rader, Sean." Josh put me down. He looked at me pissed off, grabbing my face, and turning it towards the mirror, he said, "Look at yourself Crystal, look what you're doing to yourself! If that man loves you the way he says, he will also change his life."

I knew Josh all my life. He was always good to me. He knew my background and seeing me like that was hard for him. He told me "This isn't you Crystal, and this won't be you, I can't leave you behind."

CHAPTER 57

"ALWAYS REMEMBER US THIS WAY" Lady Gaga

I looked at Josh and told him I needed him to take me where Sean was. I couldn't leave him without telling him goodbye. He nodded his head, agreeing he would take me to him. We pulled up and I jumped out the car. Sean was already standing outside waiting for me. I ran into his arms crying. I told him how sorry I was for everything I had caused to ever hurt him. He was holding me tightly and told me everything was going to be ok. I told him I didn't know how I was going to be able to do this without him. He looked at me, and said, "You're one of the toughest women I have ever met, and you're not scared of anything." I looked up at him and told him I feared myself. He told me, "We all are brat, but you never have to be scared unless you see me scared, understand!" I gave him the biggest hug and kiss and I said goodbye.

I drove off looking in the rear-view mirror, seeing him stand in the middle of the road watching me safely leave that shit hole city. I never felt pain the way I felt pain that day, leaving someone I so wanted to take care of but couldn't because I was too sick. Josh held my hand the whole time I cried. He never said a word. I let go of his hand and looked at myself one last time before I said goodbye to that sad soul. I asked him to take me one last place before we got on the highway.

We pulled up to an empty lot with a pine tree standing tall and strong. We arrived at 501 W. Kildare Lima, Ohio. Lima, Ohio, where my grandma Rita and my grandpa Max gave me my first safe haven. I opened the car door and walked into the yard I used to play so freely in. I felt the breeze running its fingers through my hair and the sun wrapping its arms around my body. I took a deep breath, leaning against that tree and I looked up to the sky. I told my family that I was going to make them all proud, and that I loved them.

The further we drove away from that city, the more I felt my lungs breathing again. Anxiety washed away and fear disappeared. I surrendered that day - putting my hands in my pocket, pulling out a sack of meth, I rolled down the window and threw that poison out my life forever. I leaned down and turned on an old Rock N Roll station. I listened to the songs I knew were signs from my mother Cindy, and my father Chris: that they were both there with me. I had a long drive, so I closed my eyes and I rested for the first time in years.

We made it to the Hilton where I reserved a room close to the detox center. I was going to. I woke up two days later. I wasn't high and I was far away from what I've always known all my life, hungry and feeling foggy. I heard the doorbell to my suite. Josh stood with a bag of food in one hand and my famous McDonald's Frappe in the other. The way I was feeling though, was if it wasn't a hand full of drugs and pain he was carrying in, I didn't want anything to do with it. I walked to my bed and pulled the covers over my head. Josh laughed, pulled them off me and told me to get up because that day was the beginning of many blessings ahead of me.

CHAPTER 58

"GET YOU THE MOON" Kina

That day he took me downtown in Youngstown. So many business people were walking to their destinations and beautiful empty buildings. It felt good to walk, knowing I wouldn't run into anyone I knew. He took me out to eat that day. I remember putting the food in my mouth faster than I could eat, choking from no longer knowing how to eat. I even threw up that night from my stomachache. I had consumed more than it was used to.

Every day that went by I found myself feeling better and re-learning to communicate with myself. When Josh saw that I was starting to feel better, he looked at me knowing that if I didn't get professional help, I would run back thinking I would be ok. He cried that day knowing that the disease we both shared would kill us if we ever went back to that lifestyle.

He said, "Crystal, I'm asking you to make that call for yourself." I knew what he meant, and I knew what I promised myself I would do, so I made the call to New Day Recovery in Youngstown Ohio at (330-953-1977). They didn't hesitate to tell me to come in. They saved my life and gave me freedom for the first time in 40 years. They were understanding and caring, and no one judged me. They listened to me cry and offered me a new way of life.

When they told me it was time to take care of Crystal, I thought they were nuts, I thought shit, I have too many people I have to rescue. They smirked and said,

"How are you going to rescue anyone if you're dead?" The nurses were checking my vitals every hour and making sure I was getting up to eat and drink.

I went to the classes they offered, to see if I could trust these strangers that were helping me. Time went by and it was time for me to be discharged. I was called in one of their offices and asked if I was willing to go on to the next step to recovery. I was told if I went, it would be for 30 days. To start, there would be no phone and visitors, but one phone call a week to family. I could only take a small bag of clothes. I thought that was going to be the biggest stress, only allowed little to take.

My guidance coach laughed and said, "Shit, be happy you have anything at all to take with you." I sat there for a second and thought about everything I learned already and told them I was ready to take my next step. I signed the paperwork and left 2 days later -heading to First Step in Warren, Ohio.

CHAPTER 59

"REHAB" Amy Winehouse"

First Step Recovery was the best move I ever made in life. I had to wake up every day at 6 am and attend classes with one of my now, favorite teachers. His name was Rob. He didn't hold any punches, putting a mirror in my face daily until I turned and looked at it. Seeing my reflection, helped me to get healthier in mind, body and spirit.

He handed out notepads and had us write down beautiful quotes he came up with. He Had me read out loud the one I felt the most that day. He was a wonderful man.

He did more for me through his creative thoughts than any other teacher I've ever had. I was sent to speak to a counselor twice a week. I finally felt safe enough to open up about everything I endured in life. She got me through the pain and guilt I held onto towards my mother's death, and finally being able to forgive her was the biggest breakthrough for me.

I went to a meeting every night, listening to other addicts giving us their time to tell us their stories of their own hell. Realizing I was no longer alone and being able to work through the PTSD from all the trauma, felt amazing. The one day I was able to use the phone, I would call Sean hoping he would pick up his phone, and every time he did. When I heard his voice, I would hang up. I watched those doors early on in my recovery, hoping Sean was going to be the one walking through them, but it never was him.

Six months went by, and I felt great. I was now in sobor living and had made some wonderful friends. We were all on the same page, working towards a better life, rebuilding the one we destroyed. I no longer looked sick. I remember running to the nurse one day when I was still in rehab panicking about how my veins were popping out. They were so thick. I never saw them that way before. When she looked at them, she laughed and said, "Congratulations Crystal, your body is no longer dehydrated." That was 36 days into my recovery. I could not believe what I was doing to myself in active addiction.

I kept close to the rehab facility, still coming to meetings. The closer a year was coming up; I had this sadness roll over me. I saw my counselor that morning and she asked me why I was sad, and that I should be happy with all the hard work I've accomplished for myself. I started tearing up and I was honest with her and told her I missed a great friend from way back. I let her know how much I loved him, and I felt like I failed him. She just smiled and said, "Is this man's name by any chance Sean Rader?" I looked up at her with shocking eyes telling her yes, asking her how she knew. She reminded me of one of the rules due to mail. Mail was held and read making sure I was focusing on myself and recovery.

She was sitting behind her desk when she pulled out a medium shaped box. She looked at me before handing me all my mail inside it, and said, "Crystal you deserve to be loved and to be happy, that man really loves you." I grabbed the box from her, and she handed me a packet of paper with a guide that offered continuous help in North Carolina. She told me I would understand once I opened my mail.

CHAPTER 60

"A THOUSAND YEARS" Christina Perri

I opened the first of many letters from Sean, and he explained how badly he missed me and how much he loved me. He went on and told me he called his father and told him he was ready for change. He packed all his belongings and put them into storage His dad came, picked him up and took him to North Carolina. The whole time I was getting help, he was too.

With excitement and joy in my heart I opened the next letter. He wrote down every lyric of the song that played on repeat the first time we made love, "Shallow," from Lady Gaga. I was sitting on a bench, in front of this beautiful waterfall reading every lyric with tears of happiness falling from my eyes. Opening the last letter he wrote me, he expressed how he wanted nothing more but to make me his wife, and if I allowed him, he would drive to Ohio to pick me up and take me home. He said, "I bought the house you picked out, and I've been working hard every day." He explained how beautiful North Carolina was, but nothing was as beautiful as I was, so if I would accept his offer, he promised to make me the happiest woman alive. I put the letters down beside me and listened to the sound of the waterfall, pondering about what I just read. I saw two butterflies flying around me, and I knew it was my mother telling me it was time for the next chapter in life.

I called Sean that evening, excited to hear his voice. We both started talking at the same time. I told Sean to slow down and let me say something first. I got quiet and I said, "I'm ready to come home baby, come get me." He told me I had made him the happiest man on earth, and he and his dad were leaving then and there and heading my way.

I knew I only had one day to say my goodbyes. My first one was to the man who saved my life and threw me over his shoulders telling me he wasn't leaving without me. That was Joshua Lee High. Saying goodbye to the friends I had made was hard, but telling Josh goodbye was heart wrenching. Like a real friend, he told me I needed to do what was best for Crystal and to always remember it was ok to take time out to cry. Even if it was for 20 mins to an hour, but not to ever live in that sadness again. He expressed how happy he was for me and told me how proud he was of me.

I cried the entire night, thinking of the possibility of never seeing everyone I learned to love and cherish through my recovery. Sean showed up the next morning and I had everything packed. Josh and Sean shook one another's hands and they both started putting my belongings in the car. Once again, I was driving away seeing another man's broken heart standing in the middle of the road, watching me safely drive away.

Sean was the one holding my hand that morning I cried, while driving on the highway to our new beginning together. I looked up at him and tried to apologize for my tears and he told me not to dare apologize for my rightful feelings I had when it came to Josh. Josh had a wife and they both got caught up in the same lifestyle Sean and I did, but they got into trouble. Both were facing a prison term and still a lot to take care of on their end.

CHAPTER 61

"CRYSTAL" Stevie Nicks

Once I saw the mountains we were driving through, I stuck both my hands out the window and took a deep breath. Breathing in the beauty that my creator made, looking up to the sky and smiling I thanked the family and friends I lost. I thanked it for guiding me to such a beautiful life. I saw the sign, "Welcome to North Carolina" and I looked around and couldn't believe the beauty of down South.

A familiar feeling washed over me - the same feeling I had when I was dropped off at my grandparent's when I was 9 years old, Home! I was home, every bit of my body, mind and soul felt it. Sean watched my every expression tearing up. I asked him what was wrong and he said, "This is all I wanted for you Crystal." He pulled up to a road and told me to close my eyes, so I did. "Don't you peek now" he said. "Ok Rader, I won't peek," I kind of giggled. I felt the car move again and when he turned off the car, he told me to open my eyes. When I did, I saw my dream house. Standing in front of the house, I manifested during the darkest of times, I couldn't help but start crying again. I said, "Dang it Rader, I ain't going to have any tears left" making a joke. Running into his arms and feeling them wrapped safely around me, I knew my visions I held onto finally came true. I was standing in front of my dream house with the man I was madly in love with. The only man who never walked out my life, my best friend and soon to be husband Sean Richard Rader.

May 14th, 2023, will be the day we take our hand in marriage for better or worse till death do us part. He's kept every promise and taught me what a real man will do for the woman that he loves. He's always been a gentle man with me, and he opened my eyes to the love I truly deserve within myself and from anyone I allow into my life. He's an amazing man, he's, my hero. When I asked him to stop with the lifestyle we once lived, there wasn't a dispute, just surrendering and willingness. I have the utmost respect for this man for proving I've held on all this time for something I knew existed, *True Love*.

The beautiful healthy life we both live has been amazing, not easy but for sure beautiful. For the ones asking yourself how do you know if it's true love? Well, let me describe my own experience. Everyone before Sean held me back from doing better, one way or another. I was put in bad situations I had no business being in. They had no respect for me in anyway. Love to them was all about what wrongs they could get away with and control. Love with Sean is teaching one another and willing to work together as a team. We don't lie to each other, and we communicate with understanding one another's heart. I'm a very blessed woman with intelligence, and a loving heart. I love sharing life with this man. I've waited so long to feel freedom from the darkness I held onto, and here I was, with both eyes open and a joyful heart exhaling.

CHAPTER 62

"HAPPINESS IS A BUTTERFLY" Lana Del Rey

With every hit in the gut, I never gave up on the knowledge I was aware of: '*Change!*' I had to go through everything that ever hurt like hell to become the joyful person I am today. Surrendering was the hardest thing to come to terms with, but it was needed. I felt my energy grow and my soul glow with every step I took to turn my life around. I learned taking time out for myself is important to be the leader I was born to be. Learning to love myself after the torment throughout my life was a beautiful fight, a fight I was not going to lose. When I learned holding on to the hate in my heart, it only kept me in a prison, I began forgiving everyone, #1 myself.

To the one's I ever hurt in any way, I want you to know that I apologize to you publicly. I understand I was not innocent by any means, and I hope you can find it in your hearts to forgive my mishaps towards you and your lives. I also want to express to the ones who ever took their pain out on me, I also forgive you. I would not have had the courage to write this book, nor would I have had the opportunity to grow into the woman I am. I thank you for every lesson that was handed to me. To my mother, I no longer have in this world, I know now that you did your best and I love you with my entire heart. I will make you proud breaking any generational curse that was brought upon us. I have the knowledge and wisdom to understand mental health and drug addiction through dealing with my own demons.

I thank the stars above I went through it all to be able to let go of what I once couldn't understand. This is merely giving my understanding to whom I have had encounters with, not undermining the pain it caused. Humbling myself gave me control of my present time. Life isn't always fair but I promised myself to always find the beauty in it. Now, to the two men I had children with. I want to thank you Clark, for protecting me from the world I did not understand at the time, the world you knew and lived. I want to tell you I know you love our daughters and I know you once loved me too, but understand - I was as lost as you were. It wasn't your fault; it was that monster's fault and I am so very happy you have a wife who loves you dearly.

 Dear Lyfe, you hurt me by teaching me so much bad. I looked up to you and trusted you with our son. I have no regrets loving you, because without that love I would not have the beautiful son I have today. You're however a predator, and I pray you get the help you need. What you did to us was sick - controlling our every emotion was wrong. Forcing our young minds to think selling our bodies was right, was wrong. I thank God you turned your back on me, so I was able to heal from it all, I do forgive you. To the man who made me, I wish you the best and I will continue to pray for you, but I choose to stay away from you, and yes, I also forgive you. Last but always my number one, DAD, I love you! I miss you so much. You stood up for me and saved me. Thank you for being the only father I ever needed; I also forgive you too. As you know, you've been one of my biggest heroes.

CHAPTER 63

"EASY ON ME" Adele

Dear grandma and grandpa, Rita and Max Cisco,

I am so sorry for ever disappointing you both. If it wasn't for you two, I know I wouldn't have the forgiving heart I have. We might not share the same bloodline but as I stated earlier in my book, blood is not thicker than water when it comes to the love you both gave me. Opening your hearts and arms to a soul that had a long hard road ahead of her, was one of the biggest blessings I received. Grandpa, you were the best man in my entire life -loving me unconditionally, showing me how a real man conducts himself to the woman he loves, and the family he built. Thank you. I miss you, and love you so very much. Grandma you were the glue that held us all together. Losing you was devastating. I promised you I would be the first woman in our family to do something big, so here it is. Healing and being a good role model will no longer be a second choice in my life. I love and miss you so very much.

Dear Corie & Adrian,

Mommy loves you with every part of me. I will never fail you, even though I have hurt you both. Understand failing is not willing to change, and as you both see I will always make the proper change to be a better mommy. You both come from me. You both are the two people who know my heartbeat. Holding this knowledge will remind you how deep my love is for you. I am proud of you both and I thank you for the resilience you both hold in your own hearts. Do not ever let this world take your breath the way it took mine. I did what I did so neither one of you will ever have to, understand me! Talented, beautiful and intelligence is what you inherent from your mother. Use it for the positive, no matter how painful it seems to feel at the moment. Always be gentle with yourselves. You two are also heroes in your mother's life, Thank you!

To my beautiful baby Emma,

Not a day has gone by that I haven't thought about you. I love you hunny, and when it's the right time I am right here waiting for your arrival. Nothing that ever happened was caused by you or your siblings. Your belly momma had to find herself and give you children a chance that I wasn't given. All three of us are waiting with love in our hearts and arms wide open. I appreciate your parents for giving you the life you have live and deserve. Watching you grow from afar, gave me strength to continue to do better for myself. I it will reflect better in all your lives. My three little beauties I love you all dearly.

Love Always, Mommy